Dreaming
the Mississippi

If there is magic on the planet, it is contained in water.

—Loren Eiseley

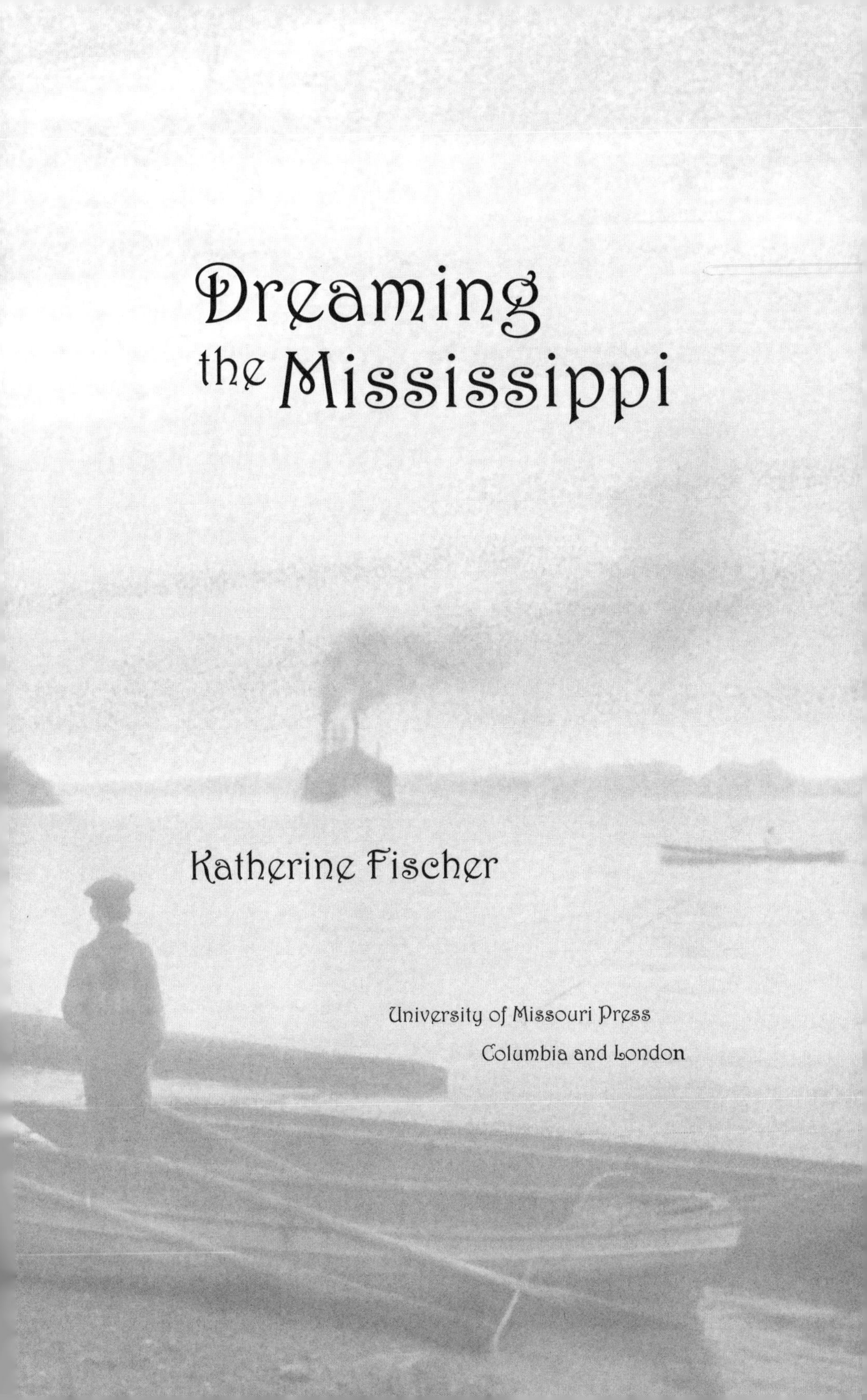

Dreaming
the Mississippi

Katherine Fischer

University of Missouri Press

Columbia and London

Library of Congress Cataloging-in-Publication Data

Fischer, Katherine, 1951–
    Dreaming the Mississippi / Katherine Fischer.
        p.   cm.
    Summary: "A twenty-first-century perspective of the Mississippi
River's environmental, industrial, and recreational qualities viewed
through stories and photographs reflecting the lives of those who live
and work in its vicinity. Fischer's storytelling explores the struggle
between engineers and naturalists, the effects of Hurricane Katrina, and
her own immersion into river life"—Provided by publisher.
    Includes bibliographical references.
    ISBN-13: 978-0-8262-1686-1 (pbk. : alk. paper)
    ISBN-10: 0-8262-1686-2 (pbk. : alk. paper)
    1. Mississippi River—Description and travel.   2. Mississippi River—
Environmental conditions.   3. Mississippi River—Pictorial works.
4. Mississippi River—Anecdotes.   5. River life—Mississippi River.
6. Mississippi River Region—Biography.   7. Mississippi River
Region—Social life and customs.   8. Fischer, Katherine, 1951–   I. Title.
    F355.F55   2006
    977—dc22   2006017452

Text designer: Jennifer Cropp
Cover designer: Susan Ferber
Typesetter: Phoenix Type, Inc.
Printer and binder: The Maple-Vail Book Manufacturing Group
Typefaces: Palatino, Harrington

Cover art and frontispiece courtesy of the National Mississippi River
Museum and Aquarium, Dubuque, Iowa.

for Mary Patricia Fischer,
my first writing teacher

and

for Jerry Enzler,
who shares the adventure

Contents

Acknowledgments

I am amazed by the contributions of so many in bringing *Dreaming the Mississippi* into print. Most helpful have been my stellar children—Andrew Enzler, Elizabeth Enzler, James Enzler, Jason Enzler, and Rebekah Enzler; their spouses, Jerod Bast, Carrie Paulin Enzler; and the grandboys, Quinton Bast and Finn Enzler. They have advised numerous chapters, permitted me to share their experiences, and applauded my efforts.

Jane Fischer Glaser from Harry Schwartz Books (Milwaukee) reviewed the entire manuscript and provided insightful suggestions. Captain Sister Joy Manthey, Anise Bonnet, and Sue Mueller Walz generously contributed their stories as river women in "Wing Dams."

President Catherine Dunn, BVM, Ph.D., of Clarke College, granted me a sabbatical to complete this book. She and the rest of the Clarke community offered their steadfast belief in the project. Kent Anderson, Olivia Archibald, Gary Arms, Jim Brimeyer, Sara McAlpin, Pat Nolan, and Angela Salas encouraged my progress even when it meant they had to cover my duties on campus. Michael Klein, Nora Mitchell, and Jane Wohl served as grand mentors at Goddard College, Vermont, during my MFA studies. Bridget Harris, Michael Spooner, and Connie Conway enlightened my revision on several chapters.

I wish all writers could be as fortunate as I have been with their publisher for a first book. Each contact with individuals at the University of Missouri Press has graced me with their wit, good spirit, and brilliance.

Lieutenant Joseph Labarriere of the Port of New Orleans harbor police spent two days showing us through the hardest-hit areas of

New Orleans down through Venice to Pilot Town and proved a compassionate, well-informed guide. I appreciate the candor of the women at the Quarter Stitch yarn shop, as well as that of New Orleans cabbies, doormen, volunteers, waitstaff, booksellers, retailers, coffee shop patrons, Café Du Monde folks, Bertrand Coleman, and so many others in letting me tape their thoughts about Katrina and its aftermath. I sincerely hope that I have represented well their feelings here.

Upper Mississippi River experts for Iowa and Illinois, including William Hainstock (Army Corps of Engineers Lockmaster at Lock and Dam #11), Wray Childers from IIW Engineers and Surveyors, Russell Tanton (Illinois Emergency Management Agency), and Bill Capuccio (Iowa DNR), have been tireless teachers explaining the many issues facing the Mississippi's future.

Tace Campbell, curator, and Denise Vondron, registrar, are the angels of the archives at the National Mississippi River Museum and Aquarium (Dubuque) who assisted me in digging through thousands of photographs and preparing them for publication. Pat Maddux also offered his technological expertise.

Executive Editor Brian Cooper granted permission for the use of several images from the *Telegraph Herald* archives as did Jim Schaeffer. The *Telegraph Herald* also published excerpts from "Gloria in Excelsis Polka," "Locking Through," "Crossing Over," and "Gulf" as monthly columns. *Big Muddy: A Journal of the Mississippi* published "Fever" and "Sho-Gunning the Mississippi." *Julien's Journal* published "Bump" and "River Rising." Firelands published "River Rising" in *Heartlands: An Anthology of Midwestern Voices*.

Thanks to Merrill Toups for keeping the coffee coming. The rest of the regulars at the Mississippi Mug Bean and Brew House have patiently withstood weekly bulletins about my writing. Caffeine providers at Miguel's and the Mean Bean have also cheered on many an early morning's writing session. I am grateful to friends and neighbors in Dubuque, East Dubuque, Massey Station, New Orleans, and Frentress Lake, who joyfully accepted their appearance in this text. Roger Powers Jr. adroitly managed images even up to my last-minute requests. Pat Kelley, Hugh Murphy, Elizabeth Pomada, Judy Reilly, and Martha Smith believed in the book from the start.

Norman Fischer and Mary Fischer taught me a passion for words and life's everyday moments. Ellen Fischer and Laurie Fischer read several chapters and asked for more. Rob Fischer regularly told me, "You can accomplish whatever you have a mind and soul to do." Although their presence on the earth was all too short, the lessons from Dora Menchaca (1956–2001) and Sam Juhlmann (1997–2005) will stay with me forever.

My deepest appreciation goes to Jerry Enzler—my favorite reviewer, the love of my life, and the best sidekick ever.

Dreaming
the Mississippi

Itasca

Having grown up on clear blue Lake Michigan, I approached the muddy Mississippi River with as much enthusiasm as someone embracing roadkill. We were neighbors now, this dark turgid river and I. I'd come into its territory by way of attending college and subsequent career moves with my family, but I did so with my heels dug into the sand. I was sure that beneath that muddy surface unspeakable things lay waiting to grab my legs, pull me under and down to where I would choke on the slick bottom, mud flooding my gullet. But as much as I feared this river, so unlike the sapphire waters of my native lake, still the mystery of it, the layers of mud and story, of a river that moves faster and farther than any Great Lake, pulled me in.

It was love/hate at first sight.

I'd heard stories. Before I made my first true communion with it—went "on the river," as it is called in these regions when you become a river person—I'd listen to anyone around me who had a Mississippi tale to tell. Each fall, students returned to our high school English classroom and told of catching enormous catfish with whiskers eighteen inches long, and of high times swinging out over limestone river bluffs before dropping in. Faculty colleagues gathered over lunch recounting the saddest tales of all, those of young people who had slipped beneath the surface, and whose bodies were churned up farther downstream. Listening, I would hold my breath as long as possible, the way you'd do before letting your lungs fill up if you were drowning; then shake my head, thinking of what the river takes.

Even as a child, I knew that where adventure was involved, Lake Michigan came up shallow contrasted to the Big River. North of

Milwaukee, where I grew up, the lake coastline is either rocky and impassable or tame and sandy, holding little to explore other than dune grass and an occasional "crick." To be sure, there were stories about ships lost during a seiche, when air pushed downward on the center of the lake, causing near tidal waves at the shore. There were mariner tales of hulls torn open, when even lighthouses couldn't steer navigators safe, like that of the *Edmund Fitzgerald* on Lake Superior. But these mostly involved commercial or military craft, with women and children taking little part in such horrific narrations. Those adventures were only for grown-ups, mainly men who worked the Great Lakes. I loved the lake, but for me, it wasn't a river of dreams—or of nightmares, for that matter.

What I knew about the Mississippi, on the other hand, mostly involved Huck Finn. In fifth grade at St. Eugene Elementary School, Sister John Mary jibbed the skirts of her habit to midcalf as she read how Huck climbed into his canoe to escape Pap's drunken beatings. Sister crouched behind the podium as she described Huck and Jim hiding out on Jackson Island, eluding teams of townspeople searching for their poor lost bodies.

During quiet reading time, I'd chant to myself, "M-I-crooked letter-crooked letter-I-crooked letter-crooked letter-I-P-P-I" as I pretended to trace the course of the river on my wooden desk. I'd imagine rafting with the likes of Mary Loftus and Mary Jane Wilkes, women "full of sand," who could navigate the roughness of shanty river towns as well as (or better than) any man. I even searched through *The Adventures of Tom Sawyer* to find the one passage in which Twain writes of a girl boarding a steamboat. As Becky Thatcher strode up the gangplank to brave the Mississippi, I was right alongside her.

At home after school, I fished storm ditches for catfish and pretended to smoke reeds behind the garage while balancing on a plywood raft "afloat" on rain puddles. Mine may have been rivers of shoal water, but in my play, Huck's islands and my own were the same. Like the Mississippi itself, a mile wide at points, here was a riverscape of imagination wide enough to include rapscallions as well as the rich, children as well as oldsters, women as well as men.

I grew up and in time left Lake Michigan behind, moving to the prairies of Iowa to attend Clarke College in Dubuque. Dubuque is a river town with magnificent bluffs. It is part of the 24,000 square-mile midwestern region known as the "Driftless Area" sidestepped by the last glaciers, which left behind Paleozoic bedrock subject to erosion. The region gets its name because geologists were unable to find signs of glacial drift, even though much of the area was covered by glaciers 500,000 years ago. The great Mississippi sweeps past Dubuque on the east, rolling down from the north to become the watery border between Iowa on one side and Wisconsin and Illinois on the other, its sister states next door. Never mind that my mother's best friends from high school days had left Milwaukee to take on teaching careers at Clarke, that my sister, Ellen, had graduated from there, and that the college enjoys a stellar reputation as a strong liberal arts and fine arts school. Its location so near the Mississippi was the greatest magnet pull.

During four years—as I majored in English and secondary education, argued over the deeper meaning of Spenser's *The Faerie Queene,* applied pedagogical theory to the real world of gum-chewing, misbehaving teenagers in our future classrooms, crammed for Professor Biggins's mega–history exams, and clocked how many hours we English majors each spent writing research papers entitled "Why Thoreau Didn't Run through the Woods" or "I'm Not Afraid of Virginia Woolf"—the one constant in my life was the river.

My roommate, Pat Kelley, and I regularly hitched rides to Eagle Point Park in order to stare down on the river to watch barges locking through at lock and dam #11. My newfound college love (later my husband, Jerry) and I enjoyed our first official date alongside the river's shores playing baseball (he tagged me "out" at second base). Although we slow-danced to the Association's "Dubuque Blues," we found it unfathomable that the lyrics fail to mention Dubuque's greatest charm—the Mississippi.

After graduation, wanderlust spirited Jerry and me off to jobs in Milwaukee, Cooperstown, and the Mississippi Delta, at Clarksdale, where I taught a trailer full of Southern Baptist students at Catholic Immaculate Conception High School how to type on IBM Selectrics, the trailer rocking with their chanting "F-J-F-J-F-J." But when our daughter, Rebekah, and, later, son Jason, expanded us into a family, Jerry and I explored digging down to establish roots in a place that we might call home. We both yearned for the Dubuque of our college years with its quaint but energetic historic districts, its focus on arts and culture, and most of all—the prospect of sunsets on the Mississippi.

Luckily, we landed jobs in this town once described by poet David Etter as a "goofy river girl." I would be a high school English teacher and Jerry would serve as curator of the local historical society. In addition to Bekah and Jason, along came James, Elizabeth, and Andrew. We were committed to raising our children environmentally aware. We hoped they would learn to tread lightly and to leave the planet a better place than when they'd arrived.

Surrounded by water, however, we spent those early years in dry dock. My time was taken up raising five children as well as navigating a writing and teaching career. There was no time for the Mississippi—or so I'd convinced myself. In short, I'd become too distanced from the very element that brought me to the city.

One day, I found I was gazing down hundreds of feet of limestone bluffs at lock and dam #11, where I had driven on sudden impulse. I heard the towboats pushing barges through the lock, their horns calling to me like sirens. I saw an island within a mile of the dam. There was a rowboat tied to one of the cottonwoods at the tip. Before I knew it, Becky, Huck, and I were again running through those cottonwoods, climbing, and swinging out over the river from low-lying branches yelling, "Last one in is a dirty yeller bottom-sucking catfish!"

In the next minute, shedding the scales of professorship, motherhood, and community activist, I stood shoulder to shoulder with Captain Bixby in the pilothouse steering our course clear of sawyers and sandbars. The Mississippi called to me in a voice muddled yet familiar, like the voice of one's mother heard from underwater.

From that moment on, I was full steam ahead to get on the river. I never turned down an invitation to go out on friends' boats. I taped photographs of canoes, rowboats, Evinrudes, Larsons, and Carvers to our refrigerator, dreaming of one day motoring out on the river at the helm of my own boat. Driving across the Iowa-Wisconsin bridge on one of our frequent trips to visit family back in Milwaukee, I would utter the scene in breathless awe: "Look at the surface today...it's like chocolate silk in a breeze, don't you think?" I thought of myself as a siren, calling to my husband and children, *come, dive in.*

I took to watching our children float plastic boats in their kiddy pool and feeling regret over my poor parenting. How could I be raising youngsters without the advantages I'd had growing up on the lake? What great natural truths would they never stumble upon, staying safely far from the river's reach? What fantasies would they fail to develop, what metaphors would they never internalize? Fantasy and metaphor, adventure and my own yearning heart—these were too important to neglect. One afternoon in mid-July, I packed sunscreen, inner tubes, buckets, shovels, and bright orange life jackets along with the children and Corkie, our golden retriever, and drove to Finley's Landing, the only sandy beach nearby that was accessible by car.

There we built houses of sand and then swamped them, imitating the force of spring floods. We swam out to the diving raft and floated on our backs, doubtless looking like an assortment of drifting tangerines in our life jackets. No matter how frequently the children threw sticks and Frisbees into the water, Corkie dashed into the river and brought the object back. Then we lay on the beach, inhaling the carpy river and watching the sun go down.

I knew it still wasn't enough.

Next time, I hauled notebook and pen along with everything else and sat pouring my attention into the page, trying to find the river in my longhand. The children played at the water's edge, creating castles and digging deep enough until the river rose up in the gorge they'd created. Corkie dug trenches for herself nearby and plopped into the cool sand.

I stared through the "snow" of the cottonwoods floating down on a jetty of rocks near the far edge of the swimming beach. I tried to imagine flood heights deep enough to fill one of the two-story buildings bordering the beach—realizing, of course, that we would all be several feet underwater if this were the spring of 1965. The thought of being part of the river, part of its mysterious underwater world, was enough to do it.

"Let's buy a boat," I finally said to my husband. I'd pasted pictures of boats up in the kitchen, yes; but I had never actually said the words to anyone but myself.

What I didn't say was that I knew I needed to get much closer, into the Mississippi's very atmosphere, if I wanted to breathe river. If I wanted to *write* the river, I would need to get beneath its skin and into its soul.

What I didn't know was that Jerry was already talking with the marina up north in McGregor about buying a sweet nineteen-foot

Larson runabout. "It would be a source of everlasting regret to live so close to the Mississippi River and never have a boat," he offered by way of persuading me to make the deal. My only everlasting regret was that I should have spoken up much earlier.

By the time we bought the boat (and, later, river property), I was eager to take on this river that runs the length of a nation—and of a nation's imagination. That first summer, I mangled the Larson's prop, much to the amusement of local marine mechanics, "Musta been flying right through the wing dams, lady, to do that much damage." What did I know of wing dams?

The mechanic explained patiently that underwater stone walls jut out from the shore like wings. When I asked him why in heaven's name anyone would construct such stupid, dangerous structures, he replied that wing dams were part of the Army Corps of Engineers' design to keep the main channel deep enough for boat navigation. I'm sure I stared at him with my mouth agape. No Lake Michigan tale had ever involved anything as deceptively whimsical-sounding as a *wing dam*.

I forged on. Excited to discover hidden inlets that even old river rats might have failed to explore, I caused the runabout to flounder in underwater stump fields, or to beach on sudden, thinly submerged sandbars. Local boaters, shaking their heads, kindly pulled back on their throttles, trimmed up, and idled in for the rescue, flung me a line, and towed us out of harm's way. My husband kept a spare pair of mud shoes on board in order to hop out of the boat and lift us off whatever sandbar I'd beached us on. My bravado about having grown up on water made no impression on any of them. They knew. Not even a Great Lake can hold a pollywog to the Mississippi when it comes to navigation woes.

Together, my husband and I figured out how to raise (or *trim up*) the outboard in order to churn our way out of mud and to avoid a snarl of water lilies and discarded tires. Yet, it would take years before I could "see" the landscape under the river. River folks were tolerant. They taught me that water breaks, furling back upon itself in a line on the surface wherever there's a wing dam, and that the downstream tip of an island (where sediment collects) protrudes out of sight for yards and yards just beneath the waves.

The channelizers among them explained dredging and the need for it, particularly after floodwaters subsided, having dumped silt and mud ten feet deep at the tips of islands underwater. Even little runabouts with only an eighteen-inch draw would be grounded by siltation. Meanwhile, the naturalists shared secrets of how to navigate quietly around nests of herons and to find the best spots for eagle-watching—while also railing against further attempts to engineer the river.

Among all the river folks, I've met characters, lots of them, like the regulars at the Dive In, one of several river establishments that offer tall gin and tonics alongside tall tales. Over the years, I've learned that folks on the river are as wild, cantankerous, unpredictable, gentle, muddy, alluring, and gorgeous as the river itself.

After several years on the river, I drove up to Lake Itasca in Minnesota, north of St. Paul. Only here, north of the lock and dam system and levees, would I find the river closer to its natural state, its primitive existence predating human engineering. Although over 250 tributaries—draining more than 40 percent of the United States, stretching from the Rockies to the Appalachians—flow and accumulate into this great river, small Lake Itasca is its official source. Barely ten feet wide and not more than two feet deep, the small stream that flows out of the northern end of the lake builds to nearly a mile wide and hundreds of feet deep at points during its journey to the Gulf of Mexico. There at Itasca, where the Mississippi begins modestly, barely bubbling over rocks, I felt a reverence for small beginnings which, in time, amount to greatness.

Stepping carefully onto slippery rocks in the shallow cool water, I imagined the same drops streaming over my ankles in their journey down to St. Anthony's Falls near Minneapolis, down through Dubuque, down to St. Louis and to Cairo, where they'd commingle with the Missouri and Ohio rivers, and finally all the way down through the Head of Passes and into the Gulf of Mexico. Only there, at the Itasca headwaters, did I appreciate fully the Anishinabe naming of this "great river," this "gathering of water," this Meche Sepe.

Since the events in the following chapters take place over several years of swimming, traveling, working, and living on the Mississippi, mine is a metaphorical use of time rather than a literal one. In some chapters, I appear as a high school English teacher, while in others I am a college professor. My five children, too, appear in some essays as toddlers and in others as teenagers or young parents, themselves. Likewise, my husband, Jerry, appears here in roles varying from

Dream lovers aboard a steamboat.
National Mississippi River Museum and Aquarium, Dubuque, Iowa

Rolling on the river.
Telegraph Herald, *Dubuque, Iowa*

museum director to campfire storyteller to faithful sidekick. This shifting allows me to be true to the moment hopefully without confusing the reader any more than I have confused my husband and children as mother, wife, teacher, lover, and writer.

Rather than a report or memoir, this is a collection of essays revealing my growing awareness about the river of today—its people and its energy as a life force within America, beyond stereotype and myth. Ultimately, it is the story of how the nature of the Mississippi connects with the nature of oneself. Unlike the traditional use of the term *river rat,* indicating a grizzled old hermit who eats crawdaddies raw while spear-fishing catfish, here I define the term anew to include all of us—children, men, and women, who draw upon the vitality, spirit, and soul of the river as our own lifeblood.

Over all, I've discovered that the chief difference between the Mississippi and Lake Michigan—and all oceans, lakes, streams, and puddles for that matter—is how it *moves.* Lakes and oceans have tides and waves, of course, but it is the Mississippi's current that leads Mark Twain to reiterate Heraclitus's assertion that no one "steps into the same river twice." It travels. Thus many of us take up residence on houseboats, our homes vehicles of floating migration, metaphor for the nomadic life.

So constant is the rhythm of the river's movement that it becomes, oddly, its only stable quality. No matter when I swim out to the main channel, I know the current will take me willy-nilly if I let it, so I use caution. I never shore my boat without tying a bow *and* a stern line. Just as life floods suddenly with events, people, snags, calls to joy and dark sloughs, so, too, does America's River; the higher its water, the faster the current. Its very unpredictability is its only predictability. We have only to steer our course, to navigate the wing dams, and to dream a river.

Fever

Never mind that our boat is in dry dock, or that it is shrink-wrapped in plastic, icicles hanging from the bow. Never mind that the gas dock has been closed for months, or that every slip is empty and every launching ramp under ice. I cannot stay away from the marina any longer. If the river is so frozen I can't dangle a toe in it, at least I can get close enough to hear the catfish feeding off the bottom—or at least to imagine that I do.

Getting past Thanksgiving is easy enough. I can usually hold off until Christmas. In a good year, I'll make it through New Year's and maybe right past Groundhog Day. But to endure through Valentine's without a trip to the river's edge? Never. Maybe it's the frustration of stalled cars and frozen batteries during our midwestern winters. Possibly it's the lack of buoyancy in my step, too heavily laden with boots and two pairs of L. L. Bean socks. Perhaps the culprit is snow mounding up outside my window—snow promising to melt, snow swearing to heaven that it will trickle down the hillside, chase into storm sewers, and flow on toward the Mississippi River. Whether sleet by day or storms by night, one thing's for sure: It's February, and I can't wait any longer. I'm heading across the Iowa-Illinois bridge to the river.

On the Iowa side of the Mississippi, there are only a couple of marinas within close proximity to those of us who live in town. The Yacht Club is pretty high-class for us. Our fifteen-year-old Larson would have to hang its bow low alongside the sleek Bajas and upscale Carvers docked there. More common river folks rent their slips across the river on the Illinois side at marinas like Frentress Lake, Mid-Town, and Bent Prop. We slip our boat at Mid-Town

Marina. Given that the river runs along the border of these states, the way I've come to feel about crossing the bridge may not be entirely accurate geographically, but metaphorically it suits me.

I leave the Iowa side, emigrating from the civilized, landed part of my days—college teaching and a fairly routine family life. Although Dubuque enjoys a spectacular new riverfront development with its recently opened museum and aquarium, shops, river restaurants and hotels, and charming riverwalk allowing easy access to the shores of the Mississippi, access to islands and the main channel comes by boat, and ours is docked on the Illinois shore.

In crossing this bridge to Illinois, I connect with the river and its temperament, both peevish and peaceful. From this side comes the passion that stirs me to write, that seems as necessary as life and breath. Crossing this bridge, I journey deeper into my own soul, where the river runs through canyons, bluff tops, and valleys of my own.

Down at the marina, at least, I'll run into my own kind, women and men who stand around the boat shop salivating over steel props, inspecting lines, lamenting about how soon until we get back on the river. "We ain't opening up until May 1," Arnie McDowell grumbles, when I tell him I *want* the boat put in by April. But it's this way every year. I phone Arnie in the middle of hard February ice, tell him I *need* the boat in by April. He refuses. I bellyache. He hangs up. I consider delivering a case of Wild Boar lager to the shop. Every year our boat is in by April 1—more or less. With reports of freezing sleet for later this week, however, I am more aware than ever that it's not going to be April for a long, long time.

"Cabin fever," one of my landlubber friends claims, "You're just feeling cooped up." True, there is too much stillness without the river rolling against my swimming, without it rocking my boat. With cabin fever, though, you're fine once you get out and get some fresh air, once you get "uncooped." But for those of us on the river, the coop is a lot more pervasive than any cabin. I could spend January, February, and March cross-country skiing, ice skating, or running outdoors, and I'd still be counting down until the first river trip of the year. As the temperature outside plunges, my longing for muddy water rises to fever pitch. By April, my mercurial soul erupts.

When animals hibernate, their heart rate slows. They save energy. Their animation is suspended, the passion in them turning from fiery orange to cool blue. If bears could anticipate spring—if more than physical hunger awakened them, if they could feel the earth thawing, berries ripening, ice melting into puddles, and grass-shoots pushing up through the soil—then, I suppose, they'd feel a lot like river people do through the crustiest months of winter. We *wait;* they sleep. That's the difference between the bears and us.

Unlike our grizzly friends, I know what I'm missing out on *right now.* And I'm not satisfied with the dried nuts stored from last fall. I wait—and not patiently. I can't help recalling crisp early spring before color comes to the ferns along the banks; June steaming into July when the river fills with frogs and fishers, skiers and eels; starlit nights camping on the islands when there's only river, a tent, and my shadow cast by moonlight on the sand; sultry Sunday afternoons when my husband, children, and I linger longer (and longer) to avoid going back to town, to avoid the harness of the world tamed.

Waiting for April, I imagine the blood of the Mississippi coursing beneath the river's skin with the pulse of waiting. In waiting for spring, main channel arteries and back sloughs swell with the promise of new life. This waiting is so like others: waiting for a child's first word, waiting for a lover to return, waiting for the dry parts of our days to fill with water. How trying the last few months are.

Waiting through the last month of pregnancy, the expectant mother tolerates the questioning of well-meaning relatives, "Why haven't you gone into labor yet?" as if there is some sensible answer. With four of our five children arriving "late," I could nearly smell the question coming as soon as the due date arrived. "Why aren't you in the hospital yet?" I learned to smile, lie about the due date, and wait. Babies arrive in their own time.

"Why haven't you thawed yet?" I am tempted to ask the Mississippi. Instead, I watch, hoping to see the ice drop like a pregnant woman's belly, signaling that the river will soon go into the labor of spring.

I drop off the latest edition of *Quimby's* river guide—the first of this year's offerings—at Arnie's feet, hopefully placating this god who holds the key to our boat. Much to my woe, I see racks full of *Quimby's* guides on the wall behind the marina counter; he will not be impressed by my gift. Still hoping Arnie will get our Larson in the water early this year, I drive across the marina parking lot to where our runabout rests along with all the other sepulchral vessels. There's an out-of-placeness unique to runabouts, skiffs, and dinghies hoisted up on blocks and trailers.

Like fish out of water, they are lifeless, fleshy, the targets of sea-gulls. I can almost see scales falling off them, their tarps caving in with snow. These vessels don't belong on seas of winter. I imagine climbing into the cab of one of Arnie's cranes, picking up our nineteen-foot runabout and plopping it back into open water. But only spring can be the savior of ice-docked boats. All I can do is pat the bow and say, "It's O.K., baby, we'll have you rocking again in no time." Promising myself that this spring we'll clean the hull, I head over to the houseboat still in the water.

Driving past row upon row of boats, I read their names aloud. *Titanic* is painted on the side of a fifteen-foot aluminum runabout that we often find over in Massey Slough, pulling skiers between the oil company dredge boat and the marina. It's a tight channel at Massey, an odd place to come upon the *Titanic*. *Pair a Docs,* a thirty-foot cabin cruiser, is owned by a couple of my colleagues from the college who prefer the back side of Minnow Island; they spend long leisurely weeks far from PowerPoint presentations, textbooks, and the politics of academe. Bare-busted Godiva, the figurehead on the *River Waltz,* reminds me of the Rolls Royce hood ornament soldered to the rusty old Volkswagen Beetle I find driving around the docks on occasion. And then there is Ike's handmade *Lily Belle;* at the tip of its bow, his barge, the *Airport,* is attached; at the stern is a paddlewheel, fashioned after steamboats of a bygone era. This craft suggests that on the river, we have our own delusions. From the humblest minnow of a boat to the grandest luxury yachts—all of them hibernate here and wait.

Houseboats are only a little less sad than runabouts in February, because many of them are left in the water. At least I can unlock the door of the *Aesculapia,* walk into the kitchen, turn on the gas, and stand over the stove pretending we're underway, and it's my turn to cook dinner. But the hallucination evaporates in puffs of condensation coming from my breath, and the pilot light goes out in the cold.

Last year, when the houseboat was given to the museum where my husband serves as director, Jerry knew it was in less-than-perfect condition. "Better keep 'er running until I can fix her," Arnie warned when he assessed the *Aesculapia*'s main needs—reconstructed gas lines for the kitchen propane and an engine tune-up. I was eager to accept my husband's offer that we "keep her running" and test drive it until the museum could take it on. Arnie warned even further, "Let her sit out a summer, and the muskrats will eat right through her gas lines." Jerry and I ventured out on our own without the kids. Who knew if the engines would hold? We were stranded only twice, when those ancient twin Evinrudes refused to turn over. That was during the first two test drives.

Arnie sent out one of the high school girls who pumps gas at the dock with a new battery to save us the first time, when the electrical system fizzled on Nine-Mile Island. The second time, we were marooned on the sandbar south of town. With a kitchen full of cheese and crackers, soda and wine, and ice cream bars, and with the promise of a sunny afternoon ahead of us, we weren't in too much of a hurry to get rescued. Soon enough, another houseboat, *Our Nest Egg,* dropped anchor at the sandbar alongside us. A few hours after these boaters joined us for Chardonnay, Brie, Eskimo Pies, and evening coffee, they offered to tow us back to the marina.

Even if you've got brand new engines and a fresh battery, you get used to being rescued on the Mississippi. If it's not engine trouble, it's wing dams and stump fields messing with the motor. At least by the time we entertained my colleagues from the college and others from the museum, the *Aesculapia* never failed.

I gladly volunteered to check on the houseboat for the museum during the winter, "Just to make sure nothing cracks or freezes." In some of the fancier houseboats along the river, the kind with heaters, people keep their boats in the water and hole up for a weekend now and then in January or February, pretending it is August. That's not the case with the *Aesculapia,* however, so unless I come down to "check on it," it sits empty and alone.

Sometimes keeping a boat in the upper Mississippi through winter means it has to be "bubbled in" with a stream of water flowing between it and the ice; otherwise, the ice will harpoon the hull. Arnie attaches a "bubbler" to the boat slip. Its small propeller churns the water to keep it from freezing. Water is the natural cradle for the hull, and accordingly, Arnie babysits bubbled-in boats throughout the winter, walking the docks daily to make sure the motors haven't been gnarled by debris and that electricity is still flowing. From a distance, such a boat appears ready to head out into the main channel—it's that close to real. But no matter how real it appears, you can't just rev up the motor on a bubbled-in boat, throttle down, and churn out through six feet of ice.

The *Aesculapia III* was donated to the museum by the Laubes. Paul was a surgeon who, along with this wife, Lavonne, found moonlight on the river as healing a balm as the wonders of modern medicine performed in the operating room. On the wall behind me in the kitchen hangs an etching that was donated with the boat and explains the unusual name. Although our children giggle at the naked figures in the picture, we tell them the main character is Akelepios, the son of Apollo, the healer in Greek mythology. He stands nearby a pond healing those with afflictions and illness.

Peering out the *Aesculapia*'s front window, I pause long enough to look down the slope into the frozen harbor at those bubbled-in boats with their cushion of water. My thoughts wander to my niece Anne and her husband, Lou, waiting again for their son. Since Sammy's birth, there have been months, years of waiting—for blood tests and doctors' prognoses, for treatments, for The Cure. Despite mitochondrial disease—which flashes upon him without warning, often resulting in late-night rushes to the hospital—for most of Sam's life, his mother and father have managed to give him the appearance of normalcy, the same way these boats resemble summer. There's always been that stream around his life, cushioning him from the advancing ice.

The intricate lace of last November's spider web spanning the front window over the *Aesculapia* pilot wheel reminds me even more that it is not yet April. Lucky spiders—at least they hole up in the crevices of a boat before dying. T. S. Eliot didn't know everything: November is the cruelest month, not April. That's the month we river folk keep our boats in the water as long as possible. Some of us even hold off until the last week of November before allowing the marina to pull our boats out and land them like catfish gasping for water, waiting to die. Last fall, our good friend Doug waited so long to pull out the boat that he had to lean over the bow to chip away at the frozen river with a screwdriver while his wife drove the *Sally Forth* to the ramp.

December is fairly tolerable to river people. First snowfall, I look up at the winter sky, stick out my tongue to taste the flakes of the river floating down, the Mississippi in just another stage of its cycle. Some of us with boats in our garages—and still enough summer in our minds' eyes—find it warm enough to finally replace belts and lines, clean up hulls, and fix. We have a tendency, however, to look at Hanukkah, Kwanzaa, Christmas, and other winter gift-giving holidays as opportunities to remind our relatives and friends of how flat the old boat bumpers are, or of how thrilling it would be to slalom the river next June, "If only I had a good slalom ski."

As brittle cold as January is in Iowa and Illinois, it's hot as hell for those of us with river fever. We try. We really do. Some go ice fishing, setting up makeshift shacks and drilling holes in the ice. Others cross-country ski. I skate. As much as this walking on water may give me delusions of the divine, it's not the same as wallowing thigh-deep in a warm current, my toes squishing into the soft river bottom. My husband, our kids, and I sled down the hills sloping toward the river, but we know we're only surfing on snow. I may tip a few on New Year's Eve, but my heart waits for the River New Year, April 1.

Humans have waited for the first of the year, hoping that the world will be made new, or that whatever was dead might be brought to life. Even in December, the heart quickens at the thought of getting another chance to start over. River people await the unlocking of the river the same way. Like a child in May counting down the final days until school is out for summer, I grow more impatient the closer we get. "What's taking so long?" I am tempted to demand of the Mississippi, as I gaze out of the houseboat's kitchen window.

On the wall near the kitchen sink are photos of the "mud lads"— our son Andrew and his friends caked in clay after digging in the back of Minnow Island; of friends toasting one another on the "party barge"; of Satchmo, our second golden retriever, popping her head up from behind the sand dunes; and of the guests who boarded with cinched neckties and pinching high heels only to emerge loose-collared and barefoot. The images remind me even more keenly of the contrasting picture outside the boat now, the frame of ice holding still a black and white river.

Plastic lawn bags duct-taped to the houseboat windows to block the sun from fading interior surfaces beg to be ripped off. The engine

Mud lads.

battery sitting on the kitchen floor can't wait to be charged. No swimming suits or Mississippi mud–caked towels drape the outside front railings, the refrigerator is empty except for a dry Dr. Pepper can, and when I strain to hear the waves lapping against the side of the boat, I hear only the creaking of ice freezing harder by the minute. "Don't come a-knockin' if the boat's a-rockin,'" we wink at some of our friends all summer long. But today the boat does not rock. It does not even list.

This stillness has me picturing my father a few years ago. With a winter of cancer advancing in upon him, he was surrounded by chemotherapy and radiation. Avid to return to the boardroom and the golf course, he seemed ready to be off, full steam ahead again, too. He would chug right through the front doors of the hospital down to his runabout on Lake Michigan, and cut through the wake of those tiny aberrant cells, I thought. A man so full of dune grass, high water, and constant motion should be unstoppable, I remember hoping. After all, he loved to rock the boat better than anyone I'd ever known, both on the lake and in our lives.

After locking up the *Aesculapia*, I head over to Mid-Town Marina's Dive In. "Fried mushrooms and a Wild Boar," I chant to Sandy, the co-owner and Arnie's wife, while pulling over to a barstool to sit and talk with the regulars. There's no sign on the joint that says "Dive In," but that's what I've nicknamed the marina diner and bar.

Right off the bridge connecting Dubuque, Iowa, and East Dubuque, Illinois, it's a perfect place for someone to dive in and start swimming the Mississippi.

Before I was on the river, I used to think the off-season regulars at the Dive In were a bunch of drunks who couldn't stay away from the bar all winter. But since I've been on the river, I know better. Most of them drink very little, a beer at lunch occasionally. The conversation today is exactly the same as it was yesterday, and as it will undoubtedly be tomorrow. It's an orchestra of topics with Sandy, as conductor, bringing them together from behind the bar. "Think it'll flood this spring?" (The cellos.) "Wonder if One-Mile Island will still be above water?" (The violins.) "Heard they're putting in a gas dock at Finley's Landing!" (The cymbals.)…No, it's not the alcohol they crave.

Rivertalk. By July Fourth fireworks, there will be luscious gossip about who crossed boats and slept with whom, about the bass runner that got snarled in the reeds over in Menominee Slough, and worst of all, about that greenhorn who hit an underwater stonewall wing dam, ripping into the hull of his boat. But for now, the talk is all flood predictions, all mechanical nightmares, all wait.

The yearly wait is bad enough, but in a flood year it's worse. Just about the time we could be meandering through Dead Man's Slough, the Coast Guard closes down the river. After the flood, folks paint orange slashes on the blacktop and trees, showing how high the water rose on the road up to the Catfish Bar and Gill at Massey. Before the crest passes though, there isn't much to do—unless it's to evacuate. I join friends sandbagging and squeegee-ing the river into drains. Then we wait it out.

That's the difference. In a flood year, we wait *out* instead of waiting *for*. We hold our breath, never sure what the river has left behind, never sure what the river has taken away, dreading the end of the waiting. This past week, Anne and Lou waited out Sam's fourth birthday. Mindful of how their son's disease progresses, I imagine that my niece and her husband wait out Sam's birthdays the way we wait out the flood—only with more dire consequences.

When my father's breathing grew erratic that April, I waited it out, too. Finally, late one May afternoon, I leaned over his bed, "It's fine, Dad, just calm your breathing—in—out." I spoke slowly, rhythmically, attempting to calibrate his pattern of breathing. I didn't realize the connection at the time, but the directions I gave him were the same that nurses had given me in labor and delivery: "In, one-two-three; out, one-two-three; take a cleansing breath." But those breaths of labor and delivery—unlike my father's—were waiting *for*, not waiting *out*.

As painful as that waiting out is, however, it prepares us, softens the blow somehow. When my sister-in-law's plane pierced the Pentagon that September morning, we were not granted the benefit of waiting out. One day, as a biotech researcher, Dora Menchaca was at a Washington Senate hearing testifying on behalf of drugs to cure prostate cancer, and the next day she was dead. Gone without the warnings of illness or high water.

For months afterward, I dreamt of searching through rooms for her, opening door after door throughout the house. I'd open the same closets over and over and call for her, but she never answered. Like so many people who survived that day realizing the loss of lovers and family members, I felt as though Dora's life had passed through my fingers like water. No matter how hard I tried to hold onto her, she just slipped through.

Had there been some warning, some hint to prepare me, I suppose, her death would have been no less hard. But at least the loss of her could have been cushioned by waiting out the inevitable. I could have bided my time, marked Dora's leaving by the clock instead of by some horrific vanishing trick.

Waiting out: It's a kind of waiting that makes me turn my attention back to the Mississippi, back to deep anticipation of spring, to the luxury of waiting for a river to thaw.

Even waiting for hell to freeze over seems fleeting compared to waiting out winter on the Mississippi. I check the calendar on the wall above the bar at the Dive In. Still not April. I linger with my compatriots, hoping to soak up enough of these river people before having to return up the bluffs. "There's a fella up near Prairie Du Chien who'll raise a house up as much as five feet. Heard he's real reasonable," Jack offers to comfort Wanda who is still recuperating from last spring's flood. In addition to making payments on a new furnace, she faces replacing nearly the entire first floor. "Don't know that I can afford it even if it is reasonable," Wanda manages to smile at him. There is a lull in the conversation out of reverence for Wanda's hard times.

Nearly all the regulars at the Dive In have been through the same thing at one time or another. When she's ready to renovate, many of the regulars will show up to tear out her mud-ruined walls and floors. They'll cut into their own leisure and family time, and some will even take off from work in order to help her put the place back together again, too. And afterward, Sandy will hold a party at the Dive In to toast Wanda. Along the river, *community* is an active noun.

Arnie comes in for his afternoon break from the shop down below. Waiting for Sandy to draw his Old Style, he points his finger at the news playing on the television over the bar, "Tell you one thing. They shoulda asked towboat pilots before planning that new bridge." He crunches down hard on a breadstick and then points the stick at the D.O.T. official just now appearing on the screen, "Landlubber city fools designing a bridge at such a cockamamie angle that no pilot could ever steer a load of fifteen barges through it!" We all laugh because we know Arnie is right. Huey Long, the former governor of Louisiana, allegedly built the old Baton Rouge bridge low enough that ocean vessels were prevented from going any farther upstream, thus ensuring the capital's position as the northernmost point of oceangoing navigation on the Mississippi. No such logic applies here, however. Indeed, planners seem to have consulted everyone *but* those who knew best—the hard hands and pilots who work the big boats—before commissioning blueprints for designs that might prove useless.

As if to show that even the experts can make mistakes, too, Wanda tells one of her deckhand stories from the years she worked for the commercial barge lines. She was standing on the corner of the bow of the barge when it slammed right into the lock chamber wall, she tells us, "Thought I was a goner." Lunch slides into late afternoon coffee as we spin more tales until reluctantly, I ask Sandy for the tab.

We're due to go sledding with friends back over in Iowa, but my heart will only partially be in it. What kind of substitute is snow flying in my face, freezing my cheekbones, compared with warm water spraying gently against my knees as I cut through a perfect wake, the sun on my back, the fingers of the wind in my hair? I check my watch calendar. Still February, but at least it's a few hours closer to river time. I say "so long" to the regulars at the Dive In, head out to my car, and push the button to open the moon roof, hoping the February sun might have melted the crust of snow on top of the car. No luck.

As I head back over the bridge, I think of how close death seems just before spring, of how dark night must become before stars can appear visible, of my father, of Dora, of Anne's waiting, and of Sammy. Having been to the winter river, I'm finding new ways to come to terms with these losses. In the rhythm of a river turning to ice and in the talk of the regulars at the Dive In, I find a comforting steadiness. Hitting a pothole halfway across the bridge, I am jarred out of my ruminations back into the present moment.

The news that came this morning is so fresh I have nearly forgotten about it. I catch my breath recalling the phone call from our oldest daughter, Bekah, and the excitement in her voice, "Jerod and I are expecting!" Our first grandchild will join us for future seasons on the river. I imagine a small lawn chair on the beach with bucket and shovel next to it. I see Rebekah and Jerod whooshing their life-jacketed, inner-tubed toddler back and forth between them in the shoal water near the shore. My "waiting out" shifts to waiting *for,* growing even more impatient than waiting for April as I let my imagination run crazy as the river.

In the middle of my reverie, I look out across the bridge onto the river below as I drive back to Iowa. There is a thin, barely discernable line cutting across the river south of the dam like the linea nigra bisecting a pregnant woman's stomach just weeks before giving birth. They've been ice fishing down there for two months now, but this line in the ice is new. This line signals that the ice's thickening is over. This line holds the promise of thaw, of a beginning. It may be months away, but nature is drawing a line in the ice. And as I reach the other side of the bridge, I hear the river—stretching, yawning, and cracking open its backbone.

River Rising

Digging the sand, scoop. Filling the bag, cinch. Hoisting it up, swing. Feeling the bag rise in arcs, I pass it along to the next in line, hands to hands to hands to river shore. My friends and I find our rhythm sandbagging the Mississippi in early spring, and as we work, we pass our stories along with the bags.

"You hear 'bout that fella down by Sabula? He lost his cow to it."

"And then there was the *Ark*. She was one sweet little houseboat. Broke loose of her moorings. Found her clear down by Bellevue."

"Bookstore downriver, too. Ain't no drying river silt outta paper."

"My cousin and her family lost forty acres of corn to it. First drought...then flood."

"That ain't nuthin! My brother lost his toe to it...sandbagging in all that sludge."

"Oh? You think *that's* something? My sister lost her virginity to it."

Flood stories of loss grow larger as the river grows higher during rising—you hear them every spring all up and down the Mississippi River valley from Minneapolis, where high-water misery begins, right down past Dubuque, past St. Louis, and into the Gulf. Even springs when the waters don't rise, stories flood into the streets and markets of our towns and break through the walls of classrooms and churches, drenching us with respect for the power of the mighty Mississip.

Despite monumental human efforts beginning in the 1830s to harness, divert, board in, and dig out the river, the Mississippi refuses to be held. Up until the invention of snag boats in the 1830s, people who lived along the river modified their own rhythms and needs to those of the river. Boat builders before the 1830s even created vessels equipped with side spars that could "grasshopper" the body of the boat over sandbanks and shoal water when the draw of the boat was too deep. If this didn't work, they waited for higher water. *They* made way for the river.

But then came snag boats. These vessels searched the inland waterways looking for tree trunks, limbs, and debris that might "snag" or tangle steamboat paddlewheels or that might tear through the hulls. Hooks snagged the debris, and workers hauled it on board, clearing the channel. It seems simple today, but this invention radically altered our thinking about the river. The snag boat was the first to make the *river* make way.

From this tiny trickle of a source—like the origins of the Mississippi itself, where the water barely dribbles over rocks—flowed an increasing rush of efforts and engineering to slim the river, dredge the bottom, fill in the swamplands, dam it, damn it. We've tried everything from snag boats to steam-powered dredges, from levees and floodwalls to people like us sandbagging to keep the river subdued.

No wonder the river is not itself.

"Could be as bad as '93, but it won't get near '65," Molly Ryan offers as she passes another bag. The stories we tell as we stand calf-deep in rising waters grow to mythological proportions. We measure the river this way; by years, big flood years that reach Noah levels over time with the telling. In recent memory in our region, 1965 was the worst, followed closely by the flood of 1993, and then by 2001, a flood still fresh in our memories and in our basements.

It's not just water that comes, at first seeping in through basement windows, later trickling under the door, and eventually, like in '65 and '01, smashing through windows and walls. It's not just that the water threatens to drown chickens and fritz out the battery on the Ford pickup. It's not just the carpets and sofas soggy with silt and mud. That would just be a matter of mopping. That could just be left to thin air.

It's what the river carries that does the damage—tree trunks, old tires, gnarled engine props, rusty oil drums, paper diapers, plastic forks, torn condoms, chicken bones, beer cans, crumples of tin foil smeared with barbecue sauce and brown muck, corncobs, manufactured things twisted and seaweeded into indiscernible shapes,

Flood ultimatum.
Telegraph Herald, *Dubuque, Iowa*

sludge and mud and silt and sediment, dead fish, and the last traces of DDT invested in animal tissue before the EPA ban in 1973.

This is to say nothing of industrial and agricultural pollution dumped even within legal limits. There are five federal Superfund sites in Minneapolis within five miles of the river's edge alone. These sites, as well as dozens more, rank as some of the worst toxic dumps in the country. Floodwaters drench homes with waves of chlorine and pesticide runoff laced with untreated hog feces, air conditioning coolant, mercury, nitrates, as well as with legal-dump chemicals whose future havoc we do not yet know. These not only enter and irreparably bond with sofa cushions and grandma's braided rug, but also infiltrate the air.

The problem is not just a local one, either. The Mississippi provides 23 percent of the nation's public surface water supplies. Eighteen million people depend on the Mississippi and its tributaries for drinking water.

Flood magnitude is measured in loss spring after spring. Human loss, mainly. What did the river take? What did it leave behind? River risings disturb the rhythms of our routines. Our children tell teachers they couldn't get their homework submitted on time because, in the riverine version of "my dog ate it," their math workbooks fell out of the boat on the way to school.

Their parents' stories grow, too, as big as fish tales. The stocky fellow I'm passing to, who wears an L.L. Bean red plaid shirt, pauses between handoffs to tell us about his sister, a college student, who volunteered to feed sandwiches to National Guard workers called in on emergency during the flood of '65. "All those men, all her Iowa innocence—she *must* have lost her virginity," he claims.

Talk turns to levees and retention basins, to sandbagging and floodwalls. Floodwalls, those nearly impenetrable barriers of concrete, fortress several towns on the upper river above St. Louis. As the waters rise, the watchers at the gates wait at the button. When word comes down from the next town upstream that the river is cresting above flood level, the button is pressed, and heavy steel gates close like bank vault doors. Lock. As if we could lock out the river's natural rhythms.

Communities like Dubuque that built floodwalls congratulate themselves at flood time for the wisdom of saving themselves millions in damages and loss, for maintaining life as usual despite the season's natural tendency toward rising. They don't need to apply for Federal Emergency Management Agency funds.

Towns like Davenport, just eighty miles south of Dubuque, sludge through river muck, reminding themselves of why they didn't build a floodwall. They recall the open view they have of the river. The more environmentally informed recall that by not holding the river in, it can spill the shores, soaking into floodplains of soil and grass rather than running off steel, concrete, and asphalt. They quietly reconsider, but most of them decide to decide the same again. They will not build the wall.

Because they have no wall, they now build only floodable structures like baseball fields. Because they have no wall, tourist attractions and light retail are established only in areas of the city with a view to the river but not within reach of its high flood fingertips.

Because they have no wall, they bear no guilt. By not fighting to keep their own town dry, they know they are also not forcing the river into higher and faster currents deluging communities downstream. They congratulate themselves for doing their part in letting the river keep its regular rhythms. But the high-fives and pats on the back will have to wait until they scoop out, mop up, and disinfect.

And the citizens of Dubuque—those who consider that the river runs the length of a nation and not just the length of a town—will assuage their guilt by pointing fingers at the city of Davenport for wasting all that Federal cleanup money. The more environmentally conscious of Dubuque know that their floodwall was erected in 1973, a time when memories of the devastating flood of '65 could still be found on watermarks around buildings in the floodplain. Although the Dubuque floodwall probably affects flooding across the river in East Dubuque, as some residents there claim, water is allowed to spill south of town into fields, thus mitigating the contribution to higher waters farther downstream.

These smaller flood mitigation efforts pale compared to hundreds of miles of levees that girdle the river from St. Louis down nearly to New Orleans.

Meanwhile, in the Mississippi River valley this time of year—in the country at places like Kelly's Kafe, where Iowa farmers who live along the river gather to sip lemonade and black coffee, a place where hard hands and harder heads wear John Deere feed–caps and where year-round the chief topic for discussion is the weather, a place where Willie Nelson never keeps company with Eric Clapton on the jukebox—the story not being told, the story that dries up conversation, is the story of "let it flow." You mention "let it flow" in a place like Kelly's, and you'll be lucky to leave with your boots on.

The story also not being told in Mississippi River cities this time of year, the one considered nearly communistic in places—like the quaint antique shops and cafés on the floodplain, in ticketrons where they sell admittance to gambling boats and excursion boats and artists-on-the-river events, and where restaurant menus promise "fresh-caught Mississippi catfish"—is the story of tearing down the wall and letting the Mississippi have its way. You talk about pulling your finger out of the dike in places like this, and you'll be lucky to leave with your wingtips on.

Talk of allowing nature to take its own course levels social and class barriers and makes country and city dwellers, often at odds with one another, close as two kernels on a cob of Iowa sweet corn. It's dangerous talk, this, but everything else is illusion. When towns like mine install floodwalls, either they do it to protect existing industry and commercial interests or they do it in order to build such industries and retail establishments along the river.

In either case, they rob the river of its natural place to flood. Holding in the Mississippi this way is like building up steam and trying to hold the lid on. During steamboat races in days long past, riverboat pilots would block the "'scape pipes" in order to build up steam to drive the engines faster. Competing to flex their engines' capacity in front of the other boys, pilots often failed to release the pressure in time—and blew up their boats. Sooner or later, the blocked river has to blow.

The pressure builds up in a river held by levees, dams, and walls. And blow it does. It damn near blows the lid off, blows harder and higher and swifter downstream, flows through broken levees, water rushing in currents over cement and asphalt pastures, picking up speed, gullywashing through streets and through front doors, gaining girth and force enough to raise the roof right off low-lying houses. But this isn't all. When floodwalls and levees are installed, they also dry up a region's swamps. "Lovely," you believe, "less swamp and slime." "Good," you think, "fewer mosquitoes." Forget those creatures from the Black Lagoon for a minute and consider this: Natural wetlands also offer inestimable benefits and great beauty.

Great blue herons. Least terns. Egrets. Fingernail clams. They'll be going, going, gone. Grasses, flowers, insects, and other organisms inhabiting these natural retention basins form an ecosystem that depends on river overflow; without it, they dry up, disappear, all blown away by a wall.

And yet, here we are again this year, my friends and I, sandbagging against the river because we see the need of a friend more than the ruination of a river. Sandbags are far better than either levees or floodwalls. Usually, they protect only small regions or buildings from floodwater, allowing the river to spill a few hundred feet away.

Levees occasionally break, allowing water to rush back into its natural floodplain. Sometimes shorter than floodwalls, levees also are more frequently overcome before the water crests. It's good

Passing sandbags along the line, 1965.
National Mississippi River Museum and Aquarium, Dubuque, Iowa

news for the river and environment, but bad news for people. The horrific loss of life and property along the Gulf Coast reveals the most compelling reason to mistrust such structures.

Both floodwalls and levees lure people into a false security of establishing homes and businesses on land they believe will be dry no matter what. In fact, we have seen over and over that, despite our efforts, these lands will inevitably be overtaken by the forces of nature. Today's engineering genius is tomorrow's disaster.

Because floodwalls and other levees have successfully girdled the river into higher channels, when the river finally breaks down these levees, flooding is more disastrous than it would be if they had not existed in the first place. Successful floodwalls and levees cause Mississippi waters to gush, nearing whitewater rapids because of our Passover plot—pass us over and get the next town, our sandbags the blood on our doorposts.

Water that should flush out and spill at regular intervals along the river not only picks up speed, but also picks up pollution and magnifies it until cities farther south like St. Louis and New Orleans shore up along a different Mississippi River—fetid, fecally swollen, unswimmable—a river far from the natural grace of Mark Twain's writing. Between Baton Rouge and New Orleans, matters grow worse. This region is referred to as Cancer Alley. In fact, there is so much chemical dumping into the Mississippi that ten tons of trichlorobenzene and twelve tons of the solvent TCA pass by New Orleans daily—even prior to Katrina.

Sometimes after a long stretch, when I have grown tired of sand-bagging, I collapse bone-weary and find relief in river dreams. I stand atop a limestone bluff overlooking the Mississippi's source. It is spring. There's no cement in my dreams, no dams, and no flood-walls. Trickles of snow melting from northern Canada and the Rock-ies join until a stream swells the banks of brooks and 250 tributaries flowing down the mountains through the forests, pushing faster and harder toward gorges long ago carved out by glaciers. I see waters commingling, pouring downriver, unharnessed, wild and powerful all the way down past Minneapolis, past Dubuque, past St. Louis to the Gulf of Mexico where the river empties itself into ocean salt. In my dream, I invite you to join me on this bluff top.

Do you see there? No, just a bit to the right...yes, there. That's the river chipping away at a bend down by Sabula. It's charting a new course. There used to be a dam and a series of wing dams along this part, keeping the river in the same channel as a pool sep-arate from the rest of the pools on the upper river. Now that the dams are gone, the water will erode the banks and carve a new channel over time just as it did for thousands of years. Without those dams, this flyway for 40 percent of America's waterfowl is recover-ing lush habitat.

Federal Emergency Management Agency efforts are headed in the right direction. They're buying out entire residential floodplain regions like the one at Shore Acres, Illinois. In stages over a few years, the government initiative offers flood-weary folks a fair enough price to entice their eager relocation. Once residents move, FEMA will tear down buildings and undevelop the developments. In short, they'll return to the river that which belongs to it—the floodplains.

Hydrologists like Dr. Raphael Kazman at Louisiana State Univer-sity, too, recommend that "ring levees" replace the hundreds of miles of levees now lining the Mississippi. Ring levees would keep floods out of towns and let us remove the long stretches of embankment on both sides of the river, allowing the water to spill in other areas. Such structures would also prevent yet more residences and businesses from building up along the river's floodplain. It is costly to relocate some businesses and residents and to tear down current floodwalls and levees, but the billions spent in building them would be offset by the billions saved annually in disaster relief.

There are no easy answers, but later, as the weighty monotony of sandbagging gets to me, I daydream. In those dreams, I hope for more than just these buyouts. I envision my friend Howie, who farms near Buena Vista. He looks across his fields to the acreage along the river. No corn stalks there. He tips his feed-hat to the river and walks to the end of the gravel driveway to check his mail. I see him grinning at the government check he finds in the box. He is being paid to allow the river to flood those fields that lie in the floodplain. This government money used to be poured into cement to build more floodwalls.

"You can't just expect folks to up and move off the river, ya know," Tom and Janet yank me out of my wishful thinking as we fill yet more sandbags. "Too unrealistic." And they're right. There are some who live their whole lives on the river, but eventually they show up on local TV post-flood news reporting, "River's been good to me, but I'm tired. Time to move on." Yet, it doesn't mean they want to be moved off their property any earlier against their will.

But consider someone born on the river today, bent on staying her whole life. Chances are she'll move off the floodplain within one hundred years—one way or another. I wonder if we could be long-sighted enough to enact practices and legislation today that will benefit the river and us fifty to a hundred years from now? We might pass legislation that all floodplain regions be returned to the Mississippi, and that we cease further engineering of the river. The barge industry won't like it; nor will the Army Corps of Engineers, and the resulting loss of profits is nothing to sneeze at. But a natural body of water as magnificent as the Mississippi deserves to be more than a series of walled-in pools separated by cement dams with lock chambers to allow their prisoners to advance from one pool to the next.

A woman can dream anyway, can't she?

Driving into the floodplain now in late summer on my way to our slip at the marina, I see still the leftovers from last spring's flood.

Pleading won't help; sign at Tony's Café, 1965.
Telegraph Herald, *Dubuque, Iowa*

Only partially filled now, vapid sandbags lay in heaps behind garages and under the trailers carrying boats. On the way to the dock, I see more bags lazing against the post of the stop sign. I can't help but appreciate the irony, that these symbols of stopping road traffic, and symbols of stopping the river's rise, rest there alongside one another.

Hefting sandbags for hours stays with a person for months. Lazy August afternoons, I still sleep to the rhythm of the passing of bags. I feel my legs heave to the motion of bagging and passing, bagging and passing, and my shoulders shift with the weight of the bag and the arc of my arms swinging to keep the momentum going, passing and bagging, passing and bagging.

As I rest in my boat drifting downstream, I dream the rhythm, the bagging it in, the damming it in, the holding it back. With the movement of the boat swaying with the Mississippi entering my dream, soon my friends and I are no longer passing sandbags hand to hand. It is the river, itself, fluid, resisting the rhythm of being passed, refusing the syncopation of being held, flowing through our hands.

The river slides through our grasp and flows toward its own channel and its own spilling. It is no longer the rhythm of fixing the river. It is no longer the rhythm of letting or not letting. It has become the rhythm of fluidity, the rhythm of being graced beyond our control with wildness. The river's rhythm—wild, unpredictable, powerful. Awe-inspiring. Fearsome. And even in my dreams, I know the river will have its way.

Come hell or high water.

Massey Station

"Wouldn't live on that old river if you paid me," Anita scoffs when I tell her I'm looking for a place to buy on the Mississippi. "Can't see why anyone would want any part of it," she reiterates. Anita may live at Massey Station, second house in from the high ridge looking down on the river, but there's no love between her and muddy water. All the same, Anita is the final word on who is doing what, when, and with whom at Massey. She's one of the first people you'd be likely to meet if you spent a few hours visiting along the ridge and undoubtedly one of the most memorable. In nearby Dubuque, she fixes engines, but out on the ridge above the river, she works at tuning up lives instead of motors.

Massey Station, like so many places along the river, defies the designation of town, village, or even burg. It's more a cluster of clapboard cottages peppered with a few more permanent houses.

Railroad builders sought out the flattest corridors upon which to construct rails and ties. Because rivers seek the same kind of low-lying ground, these two are often partners, running parallel alongside one another through the Mississippi River valley. In about 1887, Frederick Massey was the highly favored stationmaster at the small railroad depot south of Shawondassee, another small resort community up on the next ridge.

Surrounded mainly by summer cottages, Fred Massey's station was located between the river and the railroad tracks. Cargo trains still operate here today just across from Nine-Mile Island. To the north is Catfish Creek, where Native Americans were the first to settle along the banks. Before the automobile, the railroad that passed through the station was the primary way for day-trippers to get to cottages and picnics along this stretch of river.

Thirty years before Massey Station was established, back in 1850, Thomas Brasher opened the Mosalem Post Office nearby. In the Middle West, these are ancient beginnings when it comes to European settlement. Along the riverbed, however, then as now, nothing is forever. After operating for a few decades, not even the best postal worker could get the mail through at Mosalem. Rain, shine, sleet, dead of night are no contenders compared to the Mississippi floodwaters that submerged the region.

My East Coast and California friends have peculiar ideas about living on this river. Where they come from, houses located close to oceans are owned only by the wealthiest. Even relatives who live along Lake Michigan's shore jump to the conclusion that anyone who lives on water drives a Mercedes. Let me set the record straight. There are no swells or aristocrats at Massey Station. The well-to-do on the Mississippi River live high up the bluffs with a view of the river—but "without any worry of getting their feet wet," as Anita would sneer.

Down on the mud flats, however, Ford pickups, aluminum runabouts, and rusted Dodge Darts are the mainstays of getting around. River settlements like Massey boast three things in common: 1) a gas dock; 2) a tavern; and 3) reckless abandon when it comes to living on the river as is. They'll allow sandbags and moderate levees, but that's the extent of their engineering of the Mississippi. Unlike bigger cities like Minneapolis, Dubuque, Muscatine, St. Louis, and New Orleans, which may erect floodwalls, thirty-foot-high levees, and classy riverfront java cafés, shops, and museums, these smaller clusters along the Mississippi don't fancy asphalt much, nor brick-and-mortar upscale design.

Take Anita's neighbors, Doug and Carol, for instance. As managers of the county-owned Massey Marina diner (which also boasts a campground adjacent to the marina), they run a modest operation just up the hill from the gas dock. "Been doing it since I was a kid," Carol reminds anyone who asks—and even those who don't. She may live over in Dubuque these days, but her heart is in the hummingbird feeders on the deck outside overlooking Massey Slough and in the latest news from boaters who stop by in a flow as constant as the river itself. "Try the cheesy onion pot roast. It's on special today," she tells a couple of DNR officers who come in out of the noon sun, having spent the morning checking on rumors of middle-aged women boating naked in a back slough.

The Upper Mississippi is actually a series of "pools" separated by dams numbered from 1, at St. Anthony's Falls north of Minneapolis, down to 27, near St. Louis at Alton, Illinois. Although it depends somewhat on natural forces, the depth of each pool is determined by the Corps of Engineers. Although the lock and dam system was never built to stop flooding on the river as many people mistakenly believe, the depth of each pool in nonflood season is affected by how much water lockmasters hold back or let through.

At Dubuque, the dam includes both tainter and roller gates. Elliptically shaped tainter gates are sixty-five feet wide and are more technologically advanced than the rollers since they operate through the winter. Round roller gates, on the other hand, are a hundred feet wide and freeze in during winter months. Around Thanksgiving, rollers are set at certain levels to allow water and ice to flow over them. In nonflood times, pool heights are raised or lowered by the Corps of Engineers using a computerized system of satellite readings, chartings of conditions (like rain), and information about tributaries. Their concern, of course, is the water level not only in a single pool but also for the entire length of the Upper River where such locks and dams exist. In flood times, however, the dams are out of operation. Lockmasters raise the gates all the way up, thus giving the river back to its own direction. As much as is possible—given wing dams, levees, floodwalls, and dredging—it's only at flood times that the Mississippi more closely resembles the wild river it once was.

These pools are numbered corresponding to the dam downstream. Transcending the land boundaries of separate cities and states, river people in pool #11, from Guttenberg down to Dubuque's dam #11, for example, form one community. Those of us in pool #12, from Dubuque down through East Dubuque, Frentress Lake, Massey Station, Tete de Morte, Chestnut, and Spruce Creek, form the community #12 pool. Our watery burg stops at dam #12 at Bellevue just beyond Spruce Creek. Each pool also has its own river hangouts and marinas.

River people refer to these gathering places as "joints." Not joints in the usual sense, not joints that are dives, dirty shanties with riffraff clients, these are joints like elbows and knees—joints that join to-gether the segments of human life along the river. You find them every few miles, from the Dive In, to the Barge Inn, to the Catfish Bar and Gill, to Doug and Carol's Massey Diner, to some that are named only by location—the grill at Lansing, or the café at Red Wing. Everyone—from Cigarette boat racers, to worm-digging kids, to luxury yacht owners, to college professors—rubs elbows here, the river our leveler. Although we may admire one another's boats, our main concerns are all the same—currents, wing dams, water level, and what's for lunch.

Don't come to river joints expecting pink ladies or tofu, Puccini in the background, or ceramic tile floors. These are places where the most common building materials are clapboard and cinder block, where meatloaf and burgers are part of nearly every menu, and where the jukebox runs more toward Garth Brooks than Ella Fitzger-ald. If during any trendy health diet you break down with a hanker-ing for fifties-style food—deep-fat fried and cholesterol-ridden—go no farther than river joints. At Doug and Carol's, "vegetarian burger" does not refer to soy concoctions or a broccoli, alfalfa, carrot blend—it means you'll get pickle, onions, and ketchup on top of that quarter pound of pure Iowa beef.

Then again I've seen places like the Dive In transformed into ele-gant dining rooms complete with globe lights illuminating the river out front. Brides and grooms in full white dress and tux regalia have stopped in on their way out of town because the place means so much to them. River joints are come-as-you-are places where everything from bikinis to ballroom gowns are in fashion.

Doug and Carol's is the daytime joint at Massey. Stroll in anytime between 7 a.m. and 7 p.m., and Carol serves up news as thick and juicy as their cheeseburgers. Who's getting off the river this year, "all drug out tired from the floods at last"? Carol knows. Who had a baby last week, and just how far along is renovation on that cottage south of the docks? She'll fill you in. Price of gas over at the Dive In? When's the next river poker run? Who got nabbed last week by the DNR for illegally cutting trees in order to gain a better view of the main channel? Ask Carol. As much as Anita is the purveyor of land stories on the ridge, Carol is the town crier of shore tales.

Vinyl-seated chrome chairs and six wide Formica tables welcome any diners who don't sit at the counter. In the height of the season,

Everything in one place.

there's often such a crowd that we eat European style, strangers sharing tables. But you don't stay strangers for long, since Carol keeps conversation going among all the patrons. If you wonder whatever happened to the homey easy atmosphere of those stream-lined diners back in the fifties, look no farther than Carol and Doug's.

As twilight approaches, however, Massey Station changes as radi-cally as the Mississippi itself. The summer sun, defining shoreline and trees so clearly that you squint, gives way to shadows and events hazy in the half moonlight. With Doug and Carol's closing at a decent hour, activity at Massey switchbacks to the Catfish Bar and Gill, a place you'd probably never catch Carol—nor Anita—frequenting. My husband and I wander in together one night, hav-ing helped nearby friends tear down drywall at the house they're renovating just up the ridge.

Tonight the talk at the Catfish Gill is about the body found floating in the river. "Given the bloat of her belly, I figure Annie's been in that river at least four days," Freddy announces to the patrons over beer and shots at the bar. Freddy is proud of his sleuthing and seems to regard himself as the self-appointed detective for the Station. From this point on, I'm using made-up names since I'm a stranger here and don't really know folks' real names. "What anyone had against her is beyond me," Freddy continues pointing his potato chip vaguely in the direction of the back window, "Poor Syl. Don't know what she'll do without her girl."

"Have you considered that somebody was trying to get at Syl by dumping her cow into the river?" Ron asks. Ron is new to Massey Station. Apparently, he doesn't understand the culture down here any better than do I. "Nah," Freddy fills him in like a dentist. "Could be that cow just wandered into the wrong pasture. Before she could moo for help, she was fish food. If there's bullets involved, I'll bet they came from an assault rifle."

Bullets? Not having grown up on the river but instead in safe suburbs, I can hardly believe what I'm hearing. "You mean somebody might've *shot* that cow!" I ask as I notice Freddie winking at Jewel from across the bar. I have the strange feeling that I am a football being passed back and forth between them during a skirmish of bar stories.

"Sure, with bullets," Jewel answers as if she were saying "Sure, the air is for breathing," or "Sure, the water is wet." She's bartending tonight and offers a free round of Budweisers and shots in honor of "the newcomers from the city."

"But then again, you don't know it was bullets," Jewel challenges Freddy's sleuthing—and his storytelling. "I mean they didn't find any casings and from up on the ridge, you couldn't see a gunshot hole in that old bovine, not even with binoculars." Jewel curls a strand of her long blond hair around her finger as she recalls that once, as she was clearing brush from the side yard of their cottage, she saw a big black-and-white lumbering down the railroad tracks adjacent to the river. "For all we know, that old cow was hit by a train and the engineer dumped the body overboard into the river to get it off the tracks," she suggests. Jewel cuts a slim figure in tight-cut jeans and a fitted red sweater, and she arrests the attention of the other patrons.

Not to be outdone, Freddy returns to firearms. "Chances are there's guns under the floorboards of half the houses around here," he claims. Everyone at the bar laughs, but pretty soon a woman I'll refer to as Sadie the Lady takes pity on us. She puts her arm around Jerry and me and whispers loudly enough for the entire room to hear: "Don't let them worry ya, hon. We all got guns down here.

You can get one, too. I'll help you shop for it, if you like." I think she's kidding, but I'm not sure.

Before coming here, I'd been told by old river rats and a historian that animal happenings are common in Massey's history, dating back to the days when the railroad station was still operating. During Prohibition, in fact, a few locals hid their illegal still operation over on Nine-Mile Island just across the Massey Slough. One winter night, a train carrying hogs to slaughter in the city derailed, and the critters escaped over the ice. They were finally found the next morning at Nine-Mile, drunk as skunks on moonshine mash.

Talk at the Gill flits from the dead Holstein back to last year's flood and finally lights on Big Jake, one of the most notorious Massey Station residents. "Jake had the best gun rack on the back of his Ford you ever saw," Sadie takes another sip of whiskey, this time from behind the bar as she assists Jewel.

As if to prove the diversity of talent at Massey, Sadie treats us to the tooth fairy story, too. It involves the night the Gill became an emergency room. One of the patrons came running in shortly before closing time—barefooted and dazed. He'd been out swinging on a rope into the river all afternoon, but on his last swoop into the water, he hit a log and his tooth broke off. According to Sadie, he ran into the Gill lisping, "Git dis tooth outta my tongue!" Jewel and the others tried to convince him to go to the emergency room in town to have it removed, but Clive trusted only the steady hands of his Massey compatriots.

"Before you could slap a gnat," Freddy picks up the story line, "We had Clive laid out on top of the freezer in the back room with the light from the pool table shining down on his mouth." Attending to the standard procedures in any good emergency room, however, Lance, another patron and apparently the "surgeon" for the night, donned a pair of plastic gloves he found hanging in the dish rack. "He stood there just like on that TV show where the doctor waits with his elbows bent and his hands up in the air to keep the germs away," Freddie continues.

I can't help but roll my own tongue in my mouth and wince at the rest of the story: Lance held an old rusty tongs, "but they sterilized it with a bottle of whiskey." They sterilized Clive's tongue and threw in some extra Jim Beam antiseptic for the rest of his mouth while they were at it. All the bar patrons stood around Clive as he lay on that freezer and counted together, "Get ready, Clive. One. Two. Three!" Clive would stick out his tongue, so that Lance could attempt to extract the tooth with the tongs. After several failed attempts, Clive's complained that his tongue was getting sore. Jewel handed him a bomb pop from the freezer to numb it. I was relieved to hear that by the next day, the pain convinced Clive of what his friends could not. He went to the emergency room.

The tales at the Catfish grow wilder as the night goes on—and the more Jewel, Sadie, and Freddy drink. A skinny woman with crinkled, dark brown hair flops down into the seat next to me, looks me straight in the eye, and slurs, "I'll bet you can't guess how old I am." No matter what I answer, it will be the wrong thing to say, so I mutter something about being bad with ages. Without blinking an eye, she tells me how she married at fifteen, had children, married again, and again, how she's lived at the Station for as long as she can remember, how she's had numerous recurring illnesses, and finally that she's thirty-something.

Before the night is out, I meet a dozen other patrons of the Catfish like Ms. Crinkle-Cut who also tell me more about their personal lives than I know about my best friends. I marvel at their openness, this trusting a stranger so much upon first meeting. It's not necessarily the beer talking either, because several of the people I meet are perfectly sober.

Back in the city, we're more guarded. We like our fences. We keep our lives private. The degree of being reserved varies in proportion to the size of the city, of course, and when I compare Dubuque to Chicago, I feel as though I live in a cornfield. I have to wipe the country girl simple smile off my face when I visit our families back in Milwaukee and Washington, D.C., and I remind myself that chitchat with store clerks is taboo. Just as I feel about these huge cities, the Massey folks, I'm sure, feel about those of us in Dubuque.

Beyond trust, however, the folks at the Massey joint lack the hypocrisy that comes with city ways. Although certainly some are embellishing stories in order to rile up the newcomers a bit, no one here is putting on airs. Nor does anyone here keep us at arm's length just because we're outsiders.

"I've seen too much of what that river can do to ever live right on it, "Anita announces one night at one of the many outdoor evening bonfires along the ridge. "Besides, it's dirty. Typhoid, mud, slime. Can't imagine what's in your head that you'd want to buy a place on the river when you can afford better in town," she waits for my answer. Explain to her that I grew up on water? Confess that I feel landlocked in town? Detail how the swiftness of the current and the unpredictability of the Mississippi stirs something in my blood? It doesn't even make sense to me. I shrug my shoulders. "Guess I've got river fever," I offer by way of explanation.

Massey is a place where manners are stripped to the bare essentials, where it's socially acceptable for Roy to describe spearing frogs and cutting their legs off as we roast hot dogs over the fire. There's no such thing as being too personal. Telling stories about neighbors is a mark of caring about people rather than of making idle gossip.

Occasionally cut off from the highway in winter by ice and from the outside world by floods in spring, you have to know everything about everyone in order to survive. Who's got a snowmobile, in case you have to rush a child to the emergency room in the middle of a January storm? Who will fetch you in their skiff if you get marooned on the houseboat in low water? Who's good for a beer when you're low on cash? Who is likely to shoot your cow out from under you? Who's got a pair of rusty tongs? As sure as Huck knew better than to trust the odious King and the Duke and to bet his life instead on slave friend Jim and the kind Mary Jane who offered him shelter, Massey residents draw a line between the riffraff and the reliable. Of course, not everyone draws the line at the same place.

In spite of the driving assault of mosquitoes at twilight, Massey is a front-porch settlement. During the past couple of decades in cities like Dubuque, people have erected knotty pine decks, many of them with screen porches, all of them at the back of their houses, safely secure from droppers-in. City people protect their privacy.

But at Massey, where everyone's business is everyone else's business, porches are right out in front. If neighbors don't drop in several times in a week, you'd better find out why they're upset at you. Such river clusters up and down along the Mississippi may be among the last strongholds representing America prior to the sixties, before we became such loners needing to formally organize Neighborhood Watch zones rather than just keeping an eye out for one another.

It's taken me a while to get used to Massey. The thought of taking up residence there was too foreign at first, too clammy for the city dweller I'd become, and even for the lake resident I'd once been. As much as I try not to be a snob, there are class and education level differences too great not to trip over at every turn. In time, I've had to face my own middle-class manners, how they border on the duplicitous at times and can't hold a candle to the deep and caring loyalty people have for one another at river joints.

If your boat gets loose, let the people at the Gill know, and they'll abandon their Millers to grab lines and hop in the flatboat to rescue your runabout. If you've lost your dog, call over to Doug and Carol's, and they'll ask every patron who enters through the door if they've seen the beagle. If you need more sandbaggers, let Sandy at the Dive In know, and she'll find volunteers. She'll even feed the flood-weary for weeks while their own homes are underwater. In fact, when the East Dubuque Chamber of Commerce needs information about the river, the first people they ask are Sandy and Arnie, because the Dive In serves as a community gathering place.

After a few years of feeling out of place at these river joints, I've come to admire the hearts of people here. The nature of their humor, the way they face hard living with grit, a primal sense of order seeps into a body like river mud soaks into your pores. No place else on earth can boast of people who are true to themselves without guile or pretense as can Massey Station. Where else would I find folks staring into the eye of a tornado and laughing right out loud?

But like them, I still watch my back at Massey Station. After all, they never did find out what happened to that cow.

Locking Through

It could be the sand shifting beneath my tossing and turning. Then again, maybe it's sleeping in a tent with my husband and three children, all that melodious breathing harmonizing with towboat horns. The lights searching the shore for snags don't help either. Whatever it is, I don't sleep well camping out on the river despite all the stereotypes of nature lulling one to sleep. Yet I can't imagine a place I'd be more willing to lose sleep over than a Mississippi River island.

I lay here staring up at the apex of the tent, recalling this morning when friends Sue and Ed joined Jerry and me loading up the boats with the usual staples—tents and coolers, Frisbees and firewood, sleeping bags, marshmallows and chocolate bars, more coolers, matches, and ice, lots of ice. Although our first destination is officially named "Nine-Mile Island" on the river charts, there's no romance in the practice of naming islands by how many miles they are downstream from the lock and dam. So we baptize islands and sloughs at whim, changing names season to season, sometimes week to week.

Several of us still refer to the slough at the back side of One-Mile Island as "Laube Slough" after Paul and LaVonne Laube, who regularly navigated their forty-foot houseboat, the *Aesculapia*, with aplomb through the narrow and shallow cut off the main channel. My children, however, call that same plot of sand at the back of the slough "Minnow Island," because in high water, schools of minnows swim right through the middle of it. This afternoon, we decided that Nine-Mile would become Jackson Island for the week, in honor of Huck Finn's island retreat where he and Jim escaped from the complications of living in town.

This campout began innocently enough. Sue and Ed, Jerry and I, and the kids were lounging around an island after hours of boating, swimming, and tubing the back slough near the lock and dam. Long after the midday sun saddled up and headed west, we dined on the usual royal river fare of bratwurst and burgers, Iowa sweet corn cooked over coals, and fresh peaches. Although it was getting late, no one said a word about revving up the outboard and heading back to the docks. Sunday lazing into twilight, we watched the fireflies light up the island and the cottonwoods. We lolled along on the beach like the river itself in low water, slowing to two miles an hour.

Sitting in a striped beach chair, working my knitting between my fingers, I paused between two rows in the hat I was making, looked up at the mainland across from where we were at Minnow Island, and knew in an instant: I didn't want to go back there. I felt as resistant to returning to town as Huck did toward the Widow Douglas's attempts to "civilize" him. Before I knew it, I popped out with the absurd, "What's to stop us from staying out on the island all week?" "Work," Jerry automatically responded.

But when we really got down to it, we realized that none of us *had* to work the full week. Sue wasn't scheduled at the hospital for a nurse's shift until next Sunday. I was done with my meetings at the college for the summer. Jerry allowed that he could go into the office for half a day and "clean things up" before taking the rest of the week off. Ed had work and his everyday noon basketball game at the Y, but maybe he could shake loose for at least two days. I watched the idea grow on Jerry and Ed just as the river rises up the banks in spring. "We could boat to the marina in the morning and come back out in time for dinner at night," Jerry agreed.

Although Elizabeth reminded us, "I have a life, you know!" she still decided she could leave the city and her teenage social interactions for a few days on the river. Not yet an employee or a teenager, Andrew was clearer on it than any of us. Hang out on the river for a week? No schedules? Plunge into mud whenever it gets too hot? Eat cherry licorice to his heart's content? No baths!

We were agreed. We'd do it—head back to shore, gather provisions, including Andrew's friend Tim, and head out the next day for a week's stay.

Shifting to my left side, I'm not having any more luck falling asleep than I did on my back. Instead, I continue to replay the events from early this morning as we prepared for the big campout. "Grab a deck of cards," I called to Andrew in the next room as I threw another pack of matches into the box along with roasting forks, the heavy black cast-iron pan, and last but not least, knitting needles and two balls of blue yarn I'd purchased at the Sow's Ear near Madison. With the yarn came all the cheer and good karma from the shop.

Before the campout, everything imagined is always perfect— sunny beach and cool breezes, smiling children creating villages out of sand (and not missing video games one bit), gourmet meals cooked in a single pan over coals, muscles loosening, relaxation. Not even a Norman Rockwell painting could compete with the flawlessness of my visions this morning.

I knew several things could go wrong: A thunderstorm may send us to the tent tightly crammed together. If it lasted long enough, the rain might spank us back to the harbor; by the third day, the kids might complain of being bored; four days of hot dogs and s'mores can turn any stomach; we may run out of propane; and the prop could hit a wing dam. But as of the pack-up this morning, all was perfectly pitched tents and clear channels ahead. I even convinced Andrew that one last shower before hitting the beach was a good idea. The only showers on the river would sprinkle from a perforated camp pouch suspended from the upper deck. River water warmed by the midday sun is a treat, but when it comes to actual cleanliness, I knew the most it could promise was to swish the sand farther down on one's body.

Maybe sitting up until I'm so drowsy I fall back into my sleeping bag will work. But as I see the sliver of the moon casting shadows in the tent, I recall the start of our day on the river. We hit the island beach hours ago at ten o'clock this morning. Jerry and I drove the nineteen-foot Larson, and Sue and Ed had their thirty-foot Carver stocked to the gills.

Monday. The island was deserted, just the way I like it. Good weather weekends on Jackson Island find boats lining the beach, bows anchored into the sand every five feet, sometimes closer. It's a friendly crowd—glossy young men and women tanning in the sun, kids digging to China, lovers writing their names inside hearts on the sand, and friends in beach chairs whiling away the week's worries.

On the weekends, the voices of Elvis, Britney, and Travis emanate from radios, accompanying hawks soaring over limestone bluffs. Last Saturday a retro young woman wearing bell-bottoms and love beads strummed the guitar as her friend accompanied her on bongos. Together they lariated a group of listeners into a circle. After four verses of "Where Have All the Flowers Gone," a terrier and a tot in a pink dotted suit pranced up to the musicians and halted, staring up at them, probably to make sure they were real. Grandma over in the chaise started chair-dancing the Macarena. Before long a beefy lad helped her out of her chair and they danced, a can of Pepsi cupped in their joined hands.

Things have not changed much over the last century when it comes to pleasure boating and lounging on the islands. Groups much like this have gathered on the islands for the sake of recreation long before us. Sure, turn-of-the-century pleasure boats like the *Rosalie* had only a two-cylinder engine contrasted to the big Bajas today zipping across the channel, their huge exhaust pipes emitting sonic booms. Unlike modern motor boats, too, the *Rosalie's* grace was obvious in the billowing canopy that shielded its owners from the summer sun. But even back then, mom and dad packed the kids and dog into the boat and steered out to Nine-Mile. I'm sure they nicknamed it Grant's Island or maybe Tubman's Island, after famed abolitionist Harriet Tubman.

Fashion may have been different when the *Rosalie* brought families to the island, but recreating was essentially the same. Decked out in her blousy green skirted suit with stockings covering her legs, mom waded in the shoal water along the shore. A few feet away, her husband, dressed in an orange and red striped two-piece suit, called, "Here she comes" to his wife. He gently pushed their daughter, encircled around the middle by a bike tire inner tube, across the water, her braids flying behind her as she giggled.

Up on the beach, someone played a fiddle, and a young couple danced, their feet swirling circles in the sand. Granny spread out a checkered tablecloth and then helped Grandpa unpack the picnic basket—home-stuffed sausages, loaves of crusty bread, and Iowa

The *Rosalie* provides relief from summer heat, 1911.
National Mississippi River Museum and Aquarium, Dubuque, Iowa

sweet corn. Rover watched, hoping they'd drop one of those sausages in the sand.

Flanking the activity and sounds of Jackson Island today is always the aroma of thick Midwestern food—bratwurst, burning marshmallows, two-inch thick steaks, and beef burgers swamped in ketchup and mustard. It's a difficult place to be a vegetarian. You'll see the occasional hibachi grilling green peppers and organic flour tortilla shells, fresh fruit chilled from the cooler, and unsweetened iced tea. But for the most part, the cuisine on river islands would harden a cardiac doctor's arteries just at the thought of it.

Driving the main channel on Saturdays and Sundays is a little like riding a bicycle against New York City rush hour traffic, only worse. Thinking of the weekend chaos on the river makes me shift again in the tent, still trying to be quiet enough not to awaken the quartet of others. Sadly, many boaters practice a form of nautical ambidexterity, one hand on the throttle, the other on a bottle. Although the Department of Natural Resources and the Coast Guard patrol the channel, it's easier to count life jackets than to assess how many beers drivers have had. They flag down boats and issue tickets, but there's so much traffic out there, it's as impossible to keep

Turn-of-the-century houseboaters camped out on river island.
National Mississippi River Museum and Aquarium, Dubuque, Iowa

River island bathers, ca. 1915.
National Mississippi River Museum and Aquarium, Dubuque, Iowa

up with weekend inebriation as it is to ticket all the drunk drivers on New Year's Eve on city streets.

"Boat drinks," some mistakenly believe, "don't count," aren't really alcoholic as long as you drink them while on the boat. "Anyone caught fighting on the premises will pay a $500 fine," the historic sign at the Dive In says. It's left over from the days when barge deckhands frequented such joints on Saturday nights and "sometimes got carried away," Sandy explains. Like most other owners of river joints, Sandy works at keeping a lid on the amount of alcohol people consume at the marina bar. All the same, there's only so much bartenders can do to track the condition of patrons. It's not because they don't care. They do, but it's hard to stay on top of sobriety with the rapid in/out flow of clients. Besides, most of the hard drinking goes on in private boats.

I've seen drivers who wouldn't touch a single glass of wine before driving home on city roadways drink a six-pack before heading back down the channel to their marina. Maybe it's the illusion that the muddy blue channel is somehow less of a road than Main Street or that boats aren't as deadly as Thunderbirds. To these pilots, I suppose, water seems less fatal, softer than concrete. Surrounded by islands and cottonwoods, great blue herons soaring overhead, and the immensity of the largest river in America, I guess some folks feel like letting loose. They feel immortal, as though nature will take care of everything. It's a false sense of security; accidents happen and with horrible consequences.

The dangers are compounded on Poker Run weekends. Boaters who have paid entry fees to zip up and down the main channel stop in at five marina joints and diners to pick up sealed envelopes. Each contains a single playing card. At the final destination, players open the last envelope and declare a winner according to who has the best poker hand. Entry fees supply big money prizes. Although racing is not the professed point of Poker Runs, they attract those most interested in running the river with as much horsepower and speed as possible "because it's in our chemistry" as one Baja Web site boasts. Although I'm sure speed changes a person as the company slogan also claims, it's not the kind of change I aspire to. Life is already too fast. I'm sure Baja runners would look down the long sleek bows of their Outlaws and tell me that my problem is that I'm not into "mind-blowing excitement." That would be accurate.

As these performance machines take over the main channel, most of us seasoned boaters who prefer calmer waters and recreating with family become instant landlubbers on Poker Run weekends. I'll never understand the thrill of revving up a boat that goes so fast that the river and surrounding shore go by in a blur. But to Poker Runners, this is heaven.

Instead of making waves on the river, destroying habitat, and causing noise pollution, I prefer homegrown events like the Mariners' poker run. Unlike their more expensive and exclusive counterpart, the Mariners event allows only boats under fourteen feet—inflatables and jet skis mainly. The five-card play is the same, but the prizes are sillier, and the run culminates in a hog roast where families laugh over the occurrences of the day. I wonder if kayakers and canoeists think of us the same way I do the performance boaters.

But today is Monday, and except for the johnboat we passed this morning as the fisherwoman cast off the wing dam and two tows moving barges downriver, there was no one out here but us. Unless of course you counted two gray egrets flying in tandem overhead, turtles burrowing into sand hills, the flock of seagulls scooping the eyes out of gizzard shad near the surface, water bugs hopping from wave to wave, and the catfish feeding off the bottom. Counting them, there was a population explosion out here when we motored to Jackson Island this morning.

Declining numbers of least terns, cormorants, and pallid sturgeon cause serious concern over the health of the river. Their habitat reduced by the loss of wetlands due to the engineering of the river over time, these birds and fish aren't reproducing the way they used to. But the bald eagles have returned. If you watch closely for them, hardly a day goes by in winter when you don't spot at least a couple. By April, however, they head north to Wisconsin, Minnesota, and Canada for nesting. I probably won't see another eagle until late November or early December. There will be a few nesters who winter here, but it's rare.

It's three in the morning, and Insomnia has pinned my Sandman to the mat. Listening to Jerry, Andrew, Tim, and Elizabeth, whose breathing is like barbershop singers, I finally realize their quartet is complete without me, someone with her eyes wide open—and her mouth shut. As quietly as possible, I slowly slide the zipper of the tent flap up and emerge through the slit into the moonlight.

The sand that scorched my feet this morning when I carried packs up the beach from the boat now feels cool under my arches. I step gingerly, watching for crabs on the beach, even though there aren't any to speak of on the upper river. It's an old habit, left over from my days living along both Lake Michigan and Florida's Atlantic coast. There, they pop out unexpectedly underfoot at night, scampering off, I imagined, to visit some other crabs once the shoreline was again theirs. It was crustacean party time on those shores, and I remember hoping that the partyers wouldn't use my toes to play "Pin the Claw on the Human." But here along the Mississippi, the most I'm likely to meet is an occasional clam or mussel in the sand.

The sliver moon helps me make my way along the beach. I find a heavy piece of driftwood partially charred from someone's bonfire weeks ago. It's cold to the touch now, so I sit on the end farthest from the charring and face the river. Downriver some distance, I hear the deep bass hum of a towboat horn. People often refer to the sound as "the moaning of a towboat," but I've never heard the whistle and felt the mournfulness usually associated with moaning. Without all the rowdiness of jet-skiers crossing wakes, churning up the channel, this dead of night is a lively time for tows. Farther north, near Minnow Island, they're locking through.

When tows lock through with a full load of fifteen barges, the crew has to break them apart into nine and six, since only nine barges will fit into the typical lock chamber at a time. Because this double lockage can take three or four hours and because most of the lock chambers are narrow, allowing only two and a half feet of clearance on each side of the barges, towboat pilots face enormous navigational challenges. The Corps of Engineers and barge lines have pushed for years to modernize and extend the locks to avoid these snafus. Some claim that fewer lock-throughs might be kinder to the environment.

Of course, extended locks would benefit the barge industry, but the jury is still out on how it will affect life along the shore. Since 1928, when the Flood Control Act encouraging a nine-foot channel depth lead to the construction of twenty-seven locks, there's been a lot of engineering of the Mississippi, and it's been to the detriment of the river's health.

Human philosophy toward reshaping the river, however, featured

Henry Shreve's snag boat's "pulling the river's teeth." This snagging process took the bite out of the Mississippi's wilder self.

Near the turn of the century, thousands of rock and willow mat wing dams were installed, jutting out from the shore like wings at various points along the main channel. These underwater walls diverted currents toward the middle of the river in order to scour it out and keep it deeper for navigation. Before wing dams, before snag boats, there were times during the dry season when the upper river all but dried up at points, making barge traffic impossible. A dried-up riverbed puts a crimp in the wallets of commercial barge lines. A dried-up riverbed is out of control, according to engineers.

After snag boats worked the river, dredging took over the work of channelizing the river. From the thirties through the sixties, Corps of Engineers boats such as the *Guthrie* and the *Thompson* lowered enormous dustpan vacuum tubes to the river bottom, sucking out mud, silt, trunks, dead hogs, rusted lawn chairs, body parts—just about any item created by nature and humankind.

Along with floodwalls and the levee system, locks and dams finished the job of nearly riding the Mississippi to a standstill. Channelized and reduced to a series of pools, the river is silting in because these pools cannot flush out. Wetlands, flooded over by high water in each pool, are disappearing at an alarming rate. The backwaters have always provided a place where wildlife, flora, and fauna are replenished. Most frightening is that even these backwaters are slowing down, filling up with silt and mud.

To hop to another pool, I lock through. When the gate opens, I steer toward the cement wall of the lock chamber, a space 110 feet wide by 600 feet long for most of the locks on the Mississippi (in a few places like Alton, the chamber is 1,200 feet long). As the gate closes, lock workers toss ropes down the sides of the walls. We catch hold of those ropes to steady the boat and position an oar at the wall to keep the boat a couple feet away, thus preventing us from smacking into it. We hold, but we never tie on to the cleats, especially when the water is being pumped out of the chamber in going downstream, or we'd end up suspended over the river with the fiberglass hull splintering apart as water levels inside the chamber drop. Next, we wait in this watery elevator as the level either rises to go upriver or descends to go downriver.

Fourth floor, please.

Wing dam construction layering brush mats and rocks.
National Mississippi River Museum and Aquarium, Dubuque, Iowa

Wing dams jut out from shore along the Upper Mississippi.
National Mississippi River Museum and Aquarium, Dubuque, Iowa

Lockmasters refer to our runabout as a "rec boat," and in a few of the locks and dams, like #15 at Rock Island, Illinois, there's a separate smaller chamber just for us, separate from the big boats. But for the most part, inside the chamber, there may be a towboat with a single barge right alongside small pleasure crafts like mine. More cordial lockmasters update boaters on conditions ahead via our ship-to-shore radios. I imagine what it would've been like back in 1812 when the New Madrid fault sent earthquake tremors for months along the Mississippi River basin, causing the river to flow backward. I'm sure lockmasters would have warned boats ahead of time.

As environmentally disastrous as the lock and dam system is to the health of the Mississippi, our brief time in the chamber provides a comforting cushion from the rough-and-tumble waters on either end. We small-craft boaters engage in river talk about what we might meet farther up above Dubuque or Guttenberg, about whether there are storms loose, about bridges down, smooth water ahead, or what the special is at the Bellevue diner. We turn up the volume on our radios, too, and enjoy the elevator music. It's almost as if the chamber water is an island, peaceful in the midst of chaotic churning.

Before rising through the next gate in my life, I'm safe here in the chamber of this lovely Mississippi River night and our weeklong campout. With workday worries stashed back on the mainland, I can stare at the river for hours if I want to. I can "waste" time. I watch a firefly flitting from shell to rock to my foot. Occasionally a fish leaps from the surface of the water, grabbing flies out of the air. The towboat horn I heard earlier is silent now, the boat working its way downriver.

"What're you doing out here?" Elizabeth asks, suddenly at my side. When I tell her I'm "just watching," she joins me on the log and gazes at the near, still water, too. As a teenager, her life is busy. Not only are there long hours at high school with classes, chorus, and club meetings, but she also works as a page at the local library. Then, too, there are the boys who show up in tuxes to escort her to proms or accompany her to the movies. My spending time with her on a moonlit Mississippi night is greater bedrock ore than all the lead mined in nearby Galena in the last century.

Neither one of us wants to shatter the enchantment of the moon on the surface of the water, waving in the wake of the towboat. It's a moment that defies language, one that shimmers only in image and memory. As we sit here, side by side, wordlessly, I consider the years ahead of her. From a teen defying her parents, like a runabout bending its prop on wing dams, she'll grow into a woman finding her own channel. She'll meander through low and high water. Like the Mississippi, she'll decide which lock chambers will hold her and which will not.

Elizabeth's got that carbonation you find in people every now and then, the kind that bubbles into unique thought. A voracious reader, she's constantly searching out the dividing line between fact and fiction, between the world we want to believe in and the world that actually exists. "I wonder what towboat pilots' husbands and wives are doing tonight? "she asks, breaking the silence. Together we wander to the tip of the island, dip our toes in, and laugh at our clumsiness as we trip over washboard mussel shells. Soon enough, we are bending over to pick up zebra mussel shells, hold them up to the moonlight, and comment about the beauty of each, even if they are as common as fish flies.

Elizabeth is in the space somewhere between child and adult, between the levels of two pools on the upper river. Just now in a chamber, she'll hold to the ropes on the side for stability, chat with her friends, and finally lock through to the other side. It's a wonderful time in her life, I muse to myself, although she won't know it until she's much older and it's too late to get it back.

Thinking about Elizabeth takes me back to my own high school senior year, before the Vietnam War would return classmates home in body bags. It was one of high jinks and higher aspirations. We guessed Murph would be a stand-up comedian, but he longed to practice law; today, he's a human resources vice president. Pitty-Pat, who was forever arranging hair, now serves as a dental hygienist. Destined for Dick Clark's Bandstand dance circuit, Weens sells insurance. Kerry, always a champion of stability, now is vice president of sales for a medical supply company. Lexy, cheerleader par excellence, is the principal at an elementary school. Even track star Truss ended up CEO of Tempurpedic Sleep Systems. I would have been voted least likely to become a writer and teacher.

Jim Wheeler, alone, grew up to be exactly what he said he would at eighteen—an orthopedic surgeon. Wheels, as we called him, the smartest kid graduated by Dominican High School, was also one of the wiliest. Although there's no proof, rumor had it that he master-minded the best pranks during our four-year internment. Most notable was chaining closed the doors between floors one minute before the bell rang for passing.

For a few seconds, we students stood shocked that we couldn't pass between floors. We worried about being late for the next class and about detentions being doled out. But when we realized every-one was in the same boat, and that surely school administrators were not responsible for doors being chained closed, awareness of the prank grew on us. Each floor of the school became its own lock chamber with students chatting about quizzes and this or that teacher's homework. Finally, the maintenance staff hacksawed the chains open, and we went along to our next classes, laughing all the way, grateful for the respite from the daily schedule.

Gruesome images of students charred to death as the school went up in smoke were delivered over the PA system as "those trouble-makers" were blamed. In our youth, we were sure this was a bogus guilt trip, so we rolled our eyes. Wheels, however, sat stone-faced in the front of Sister Dora's Latin class nodding vehement agree-ment with the principal's voice surging into the room. Like every-thing in his life, including this prank involving over two thousand students and teachers, he conducted his orthopedic practice ener-getically, achieving national acclaim for knee surgery.

I think of how startled I was when Murph called to tell me that Wheels died suddenly of a heart attack, even though he was in good enough physical shape to still fit into his letter jacket. We all went home for his funeral. Well, not all of us. Christine couldn't make it. She and Bob both died of illnesses in their thirties. Mark didn't make it either—a car crash when he was nineteen. Jim drowned years ago. The list sadly grew as we remembered these classmates as well.

Afterward at the Wheeler house, where we'd spent hours ham-mering out talent show skits about Eddie Haskell, Ward, and June, we claimed we could see where bark had grown around the scar left by Hoeller's fender thirty-three years ago. The milk chute, still nailed shut from when Mr. Wheeler caught Wheels sneaking into the house past curfew, looked too slim for any of us to fit through now.

We were locking through those years, safe in the chamber of teenage camaraderie. Rough waters lay ahead as we glided out to the high side of the chamber upon graduation, but we didn't know it at the time. Over time, one of our group wrestled with horse-betting, another drank too much. Some suffered the breakups of marriages and the deaths of children. In one way or another, we all floundered until calmer water in the next lock floated us into lives that might be described as nearly respectable.

Finally, Elizabeth and I give the tent another try. She grows silent before hitting the sleeping bag. Growing sleepy, I, too, feel the sand beneath me moving in waves, soft and rhythmical. Before long, not even the towboat horns—or the barbershop quartet—can keep me awake.

It's morning and Jerry is first out of the tent. By the time I step out into the chill day, he's rekindled last night's fire. Sue and Ed have left the cozy confines of the cuddy on their Carver and are frying eggs and bacon in our trusty cast-iron pan. Attempting to squeeze through the flap at the same time, Andrew and Tim pop out of their pup tent, electric with greeting the sun and chasing gulls at the water's edge. Although Beth sleeps in, the rest of us are done with breakfast in no time, our appetites fired by the promise of a day on the river.

Jerry and Ed take off in the Larson to town to put things to rest at their offices. Ignoring dishes and cleanup, Sue and I haul out lawn chairs from the deck of the Carver and grab knitting needles. We pull up to the edge of the water on the island and bury our toes into the sand. The early sun is perfect for knitting, and we're not going to waste it. Sue has a red and white striped sweater on her needles for her grandson, and I'm still working on the royal blue hat I'm making for Elizabeth. There's something about knitting on the beach I've always found attractive, in spite of getting sand in the yarn. Needles full of wool becoming thick hats, socks, and mittens, ready for the heaviest snowfall, make the sand between my toes warmer, and the promise of a cool dip in the river all the more refreshing.

Andrew and Tim have wandered to the far end of the island in search of wild boar, alligators, and tigers. That these don't live on the Upper Mississippi means nothing to them. Imagination kindles

Ribsy's Stocking Cap
For knitting on the beach in summer

Materials
—1 skein worsted yarn (wool, cotton, silk, mohair, etc.)
—2 pair circular needles, size 7 (or, if you prefer to knit flat and sew a seam, 1 pair of size 7 knitting needles)
—Gauge: 5 stitches = 1"

Directions
—Dig your toes into the sand and cast on 80 stitches (for a snug-fitting hat that rolls at the brim).
—Knit one row and join, being careful not to twist. Place marker to indicate starting point.
—On the next row, knit and distribute stitches evenly on two circular needles.
—Knit in the round for 5.5" (stockinette stitch).
—Decrease round 1: Starting at the marker, (k8, k2tog) until the end (72 stitches).
—Knit 3 rounds.
—Decrease round 2: Starting at marker, (k7, k2tog) until the end (64 stitches).
—Knit 2 rounds.
—Decrease round 3: Starting at marker, (k6, k2tog) until the end (56 stitches).
—Knit 2 rounds.
—Decrease round 4: Starting at marker, (k5, k2tog) until the end (48 stitches).
—Knit 1 round.
—Decrease round 5: Starting at marker, (k4, k2tog) until the end (40 stitches).
—Knit 1 round.
—Decrease round 6: Starting at marker (k3, k2tog) until the end (32 stitches).
—Decrease round 7: Starting at marker (k2, k2tog) until the end (22 stitches).
—Last round: k2tog around.
—Cut the yarn to 7". Using a tapestry needle, draw yarn through remaining stitches and to wrong side. Weave in ends.

their world as surely as last night's coals were fanned into light for our breakfast fire.

Before long, they show up tugging lines tied to driftwood across the sand. Pointing to the mud and seaweed encrusted on the wood, Andrew declares, "We got some dinner!" Of course, he sees it as the carcass of a buffalo, I have no doubt. Their feet have disappeared beneath the mud caking their toes.

This, too, is a locking through chamber for Andrew and Tim. They're ten now; next year they'll enter junior high. Their carefree Huck Finn days are numbered, Sue and I muse between knit and purl. Then again, Twain's Huck, with his abusive Pap and his consternation over the slave Jim's situation, wasn't as carefree as we tend to popularize him to be.

Watching Andrew and Tim, I can't help but see the layers of his oldest sister's and brother's childhoods. At five, Jason would call me from my papers and gradebook in to the backyard to marvel: "Look at the pie I made. Do you want a piece?" Together we'd stare down at a glop of mud, grass, and rocks. It was a work of art, but thankfully, he didn't actually expect me to eat it. Andrew's older sister, Bekah, too, often found fairies in the yard on the wings of fireflies. Unfettered by the rules of reality, kids offer a fanciful version of life. Who is to say theirs is any less real?

As I admire Andrew and Tim's catch, I also see Elizabeth emerging from the reeds. She's been out collecting nature, herself. "Try knitting these," she challenges Sue, as she hands over armloads of dune grass and cottonwood puffs. She believes we can spin something flaxenly Rapunzel for her. Before long, Beth has selected two slim sticks from the dunes, whittled off bumps with a pocket knife, and attempts to knit the grass herself, laughing all the while.

"Last one in is a slimy eel," Tim yells at Andrew as the two of them dash into the water to wash off. Although they're both good swimmers, I insist they return to shore to strap on life jackets before wading. "Washing off" is a misnomer when it comes to their real intent. No sooner do they cinch the last ties on the jackets, but they flop and roll their wet bodies in the sand. They jump up grinning, as coated as two corn dogs at the state fair.

Elizabeth, Sue, and I spend the afternoon lazily—strolling the beach to study zebra mussels and shells, reading novels on the shore as we sit with our legs reaching out into the Mississippi, tracking

The author and her son Andrew at Minnow Island.

turtles making their way up the dunes to lay eggs, and, of course, knitting. Andrew and Tim continue as brave adventurers through the cottonwoods, making traps out of sticks and weeds for the monsters of the forest. The longer we are on the island, the more the mud creeps up the lads, civilization shrinking back as it does.

With the afternoon slipping away, momentarily I think about dinner preparations, but this is not the time for routine chores, I decide. Stashing Elizabeth's blue hat back into my bag, I shift to begin a pair of merino wool socks in stripes of navy, garnet, and deep purple. This yarn came from Fiber Wild in Galena, upstream from us. It's a rich river yarn, and I relish its texture. Knitting socks may seem mundane to some, but I find it grounding. Months from now, when I'm knee-deep shoveling winter off our midwestern sidewalks, I'll feel these woolly stitches down in my toes, and before I know it, I'll be back on this beach.

With the sun still fairly high in the early evening sky, Ed and Jerry come motoring across the channel in the runabout, but even from a distance, I see a third in the boat. Jerry has convinced our son James that he'd enjoy a campfire dinner, so he's joined them after a long day on the job. As he comes to the bow, he laughs, telling us, "The guys on the job say they're coming to Sunday's performance to throw spitballs." Apparently his coworkers at the construction site have never before worked with a classical opera singer. He flings his hard hat into the back of the boat, however, as if to leave it all behind. So, too, I see Jerry unlace his wingtips and Ed loosen his tie before they hop out to tie up. Like river snakes shedding their skin, each of them sheds the city.

They haul the boat farther up on the beach and tie lines at both ends to anchor. I watch James—his jeans wet around the ankles as his toes dig into the shore, his t-shirt spelling out "Conlon Construction" across his back, and his hair unruly in the river wind—and think of how different today is than tomorrow will be for him. He aspires to sing opera wherever they'll allow him one day—either that, or teach high school math. It's a long road for bass-baritones whose voices don't fully "come in" until their thirties. After college, he'll have years more of schooling, interning, and traveling in order to understudy in every small town theater in America and in Europe. If he goes the teacher route, he'll have to move on to graduate school and jump through the hoops of certification.

Up until now, he's been surrounded by generous, kind people, both in performance and in his quest for numbers, but the professional opera and education worlds are not always so gentle. Even after achieving his dream, those waters of career performance can be tumultuous and unsettling even as they provide him the ride of his life.

This summer, he works construction alongside straightforward men who have nicknamed him "opera boy" and "the kid," but who have also made it clear they respect his industriousness. In the midst of all the razzing, their one continuous speech is to encourage him to finish school and earn a college degree. He's been able to get away from the halls of academe by spending the summer expanding his triceps instead of his vocal cords and equations. I think it's a relief, this change from intellectual to physical, a rest much like steering the boat into the calm waters of a lock chamber. Although he won't stay on the island the week with us, for this one night, he's in our chamber, and the party's just beginning.

Just as Jerry and I are about to peel potatoes because it's our night to cook, I whiff the aroma of burnt sugar wafting over from beyond the next sand hill. James and Elizabeth have already built a fire, but instead of a skillet full of hash browns, broccoli, and ham, they've skewered marshmallows on sticks stuck into the sand over the flames. "Life's short," Elizabeth quotes. "Eat dessert first."

As nutritionally disastrous as those marshmallows are any time, especially before dinner, and as much as I'm supposed to make sure

Sue locking through.

they don't go primitive just because we're on an island, Elizabeth's words strike a chord deep within the recesses of my own heart. Life *is* short.

As our campfire burns orange, the night surrounding it growing blacker by the minute, I wander over to the coolers twenty feet away to get a bottle of mineral water. Jerry is telling one of his ghost stories, and from this distance, I see his arms flailing in the air. I recognize this point in the story. The bear will jump out of the woods and say something unexpected like, "Does anyone have a light?" Sue and Ed will laugh generously. Tim will look at his friend's dad as if to say, "Are you nuts?" Andrew, Elizabeth, and James will scrunch up their noses, raise their eyebrows, and in perfect harmony groan "Oh, Dad."

For this one moment as they sit spellbound, however, I watch their shadows lean forward into his story. It is as if this moment has slowed down nearly to the complete suspension of movement, a moment held still in time. And in this moment I realize that this night on the island is not only precious for the splendor it offers us right now as a family and as friends. It is also a moment that will bolster us as we rise through the next gates after locking through.

Wing Dams

I fly over them without even knowing it. Finally again at the wheel of our nineteen-foot runabout, I take the Mississippi throttle down—well, as throttled as a ten-year old boat can go. River on the rise, it'll be cresting soon. The month of June pools into storm sewers, eventually heading for the Mississippi, becoming river. In October, the river recedes until I can see the telltale signs more clearly now, the long thin lines of water folding back upon themselves, jutting out from the tips of islands. Find a red pointed "nun" buoy across from the end of an island, and you'll spot one of them, too. Wing dam!

Wing dams are brush and stone walls created as early attempts to control the river. Brush was laid flat and tied together into large mats. These mats were placed on the river's surface extending from shore, usually at a ninety-degree angle extending from the riverbank toward the channel like wings. Workers then loaded the matted layer with rocks, thus sinking it to just below the surface. Then another mat layer was placed on top of the previous and more rocks lobbed onto it. So it went until the dam was completed. Built close together, often with only a few hundred feet between them, there are thousands on the river. Although these structures were built more than a hundred years ago, they're still common on the Upper Mississippi.

Not only do they divert water to the channel, but they also re-direct boaters as well, the only equalizer between the big boats and the runabouts. I spend the weekend camping on Minnow Island watching pontoon boats, johnboats, houseboats, runabouts, and the magnificent *Delta Queen* stern-wheeler—all boats with more than a two-foot draw. They make their way downstream minding the wing dams.

Before wing dams, the river flowed free, often on its own course. Like it or not, as I look out from the docks at the twilight sun burning into the horizon of the Mississippi, I know that they are here to stay. Will I avoid them entirely, crawling along the edges of the back sloughs, hugging close to shore, never again to take the main channel downstream to Bellevue and Sabula or up to McGregor and St. Paul? Corps of Engineers river maps charting the location of many of them help me steer clear. It's better to see trouble ahead and take precautions than to roll merrily along and get into trouble.

The Mississippi isn't the only place you'll find wing dams, of course. Such simple technology has proven useful the world over in diverting water. Wing dams are so simple, in fact, and so persistent in doing their job for over a century, that you'd easily forget they're there—except, of course, when you bend the prop on one.

As much as I recognize that wing dams are merely stone walls, there's a paradox about them I can't help but apply to life on the Mississippi. For one thing, as wings, they offer habitat favorable to bottom-feeding fish like catfish and white suckers. But since fishers also know the scaly critters are likely to lurk by the dam, it's anything but a safe harbor for them. Wing dams constrict the river, but this restriction is also what gives wings to boaters navigating through a nine-foot channel. When it comes to women who live on this river, some of us, too, encounter restrictions and stereotypes that ultimately give way so we can take wing.

The pages of literature and history render countless encounters with crafty lads eager to get out on the Mississippi, and roustabout ne'er-do-wells, smoking cigars as they dawdle at the docks. One-eyed gamblers and blue-cussing steamboat captains are as vividly imprinted on the American psyche as the gun-toting cowboys of the Wild West are. But women are part of this river story, too, and they're not the fragile namby-pambies, twisting lace handkerchiefs between their fingers as they wait on shore for their men to return.

I invite you to meet three river women who have each encountered wing dams on the river and in life. Joy Manthey rode the streetcar to the end of Canal Street in New Orleans daily just to get a whiff of the big boats. Now a towboat pilot and religious sister, she tells of navigating alongside men as one of the first women licensed to pilot the Mississippi in the twentieth century. Sue Mueller Walz was born into river life and has been running the main channel at five, fifteen, and fifty. And Anise Bonnet, at eighty-one, recalls earlier days growing up on the river and managing a family cottage resort community.

All three women reveal the grace, humor, and temerity born of the Mississippi itself. Their stories are far more vibrant and eloquent than I could have ever created. These are their stories in their own words.

Sister Mary Captain: Joy Manthey

My interest in the river started when I was in fourth grade. For ten cents, I'd take the bus to the end of the line at Canal Street in New Orleans. There I'd find the steamer *President* docked. They'd let me on free if I cleaned up the popcorn machine at the end of the cruise. In fifth grade, I worked as cashier and souvenir salesperson on the boat. I'd be out of the house by 7 a.m. to get to the boat by 8. I was the seventh of ten kids, so I had a certain amount of freedom.

I met Donna Streckfus on that boat. I was related to that family, a well-known steamboat family who'd had excursion boats back in the nineteenth century. My grandmother, my daddy's mother, was Anna Mae Streckfus. I'd never heard much about our history with Streckfus Steamers until one day when I came home from cleaning up at the *President* and told my dad where I'd been. Then the stories came out. I didn't even know we were related to the Streckfus line until then. Excursion boats must have been in my blood.

Some of the greatest fun happened alongside some of the longest work shifts back when I was young. On the *President* and the *Admiral,* we had great parties for the New Orleans Jazz Festivals, the last weekend in April and the first weekend in May. These are huge festivals, with musicians like Fats Domino and B. B. King playing right on the boat just a few feet from where I stood.

You'd have a boat full of 3,600–4,000 passengers exit, and then we'd have an hour to clean before the next full load of passengers came on board. We'd been working twenty-hour shifts. Being able to hear those musicians was a wonderful payoff for all those long hours. They were fun, hectic times. Louis Armstrong used to say he

loved to play on the Streckfus boats because they had the best musicians. So when I'd hear Irma Thomas, Clarence "Frogman" Henry,
Allen Touissant, and B. B. King, I'd think to myself that these were
the best jazz and blues musicians of the 1970s and 1980s.

These musicians continued an excursion boat tradition as far back
as 1884. People like the Neville Brothers were just kids in the band
when I was a kid working the bar, shoveling ice, serving Cokes, and
getting setups. We were all a bunch of thirteen-year-olds growing
up together on the boats.

I never stayed on a boat overnight until the day after high school
graduation, when I rode the steamer *Admiral* back up to St. Louis.
It was my graduation present that my parents allowed me do that.

Before I graduated from Louisiana State U. in 1979 with a degree
in general studies, I came home every weekend to work the boats.
There were big dance bands on Saturday nights. Often on Sunday
nights, we had the African American charters. I'd be one of just a
handful of whites on board. It was good experience for me. Later it
was the rock bands.

I got my first license in 1978 when I was twenty-one years old. It
took me a year of studying on my own to pass. Parts of the test were
really stupid. There was a question asking how I'd navigate in a ty-
phoon, and there I was, trying for a license for the Mississippi
River. Another asked how I'd navigate *around* a hurricane on the
ocean, and I thought to myself that on the Mississippi, you're stuck,
there's no way getting *around* it. One item even asked about piloting
around ice floes. You don't go north into ice on the river, so
it didn't make any sense to me in considering a riverboat captain
license. After the test, I wrote letters to the admiral of the Coast
Guard telling him they were stupid questions. Eventually, they
dropped some of them out of the test.

I was the only woman pilot out there, but I felt a connection with
the women who worked with their husbands as pilots during the
nineteenth century. I didn't think much about being the only woman
piloting on the river initially. Except for one teacher in grade school,
who'd tried to convince me I couldn't be a pilot because I was a
girl, I'd had plenty of support in becoming a captain. The male captains I'd known were very encouraging.

I'd steered boats back when I was ten years old. The captain on
the *Mark Twain*, during five-hour bayou cruises, would let me stay

up in the pilothouse the whole trip. He'd slide a steel milk crate over to the wheel for me, so I could stand on it to navigate. He'd be right there eating his sandwich and pie. He'd let me turn the boat around, too. He knew I wanted to be a pilot, so he'd help me along. Steering the big boats is just like steering a little boat. Once you get up there into the pilothouse, you just do it. There's nothing to it. Anyone could do it.

All the guys on the excursion boats were great. One of the captains who had earlier piloted the *Sprague* was an old-timer, T. Jay Decreaux. He was 100 percent behind me. Then old-timers on the *Mississippi Queen* would let me steer, too. The steering sticks on the *Admiral* were higher than the sticks on the *President.* Captain Pete piloted the *Admiral.* He had bursitis, so he had trouble steering the boat. It hurt him. I was his cub pilot. That's why I got to steer the boat.

But once I got my license, and I was out piloting by myself, I realized there were other men who thought differently. On the radio, I'd get all kinds of feedback from male pilots who would say stuff like, "You should be home barefoot and pregnant." They just weren't used to me, a woman, being out there, especially on the big boats.

It was on the towboats when I really ran into opposition. I started piloting tows in 1995 after trying for fourteen years to get a job on them. They wouldn't hire me because I was female. They'd tell me I was overqualified or they'd question if I could do the job, but there I was with an unlimited license, which meant I could pilot anything coming up the river, whether it was an aircraft carrier or a freighter. Finally, I got a call to pilot for a company I'd done some work for before. I quit my other job, which was a lot more lucrative, because I'd always wanted to work a towboat. I'd always thought it was the most fascinating thing in the world to pilot those big boats with all the barges. It was an adrenaline rush!

The hardest thing on the tows for crewmen was when I became their supervisor. They just weren't used to having a woman in charge. Once I was working the tows, though, there wasn't any question if I could handle things as a female. I was pushing one of the biggest tows on the canal with one of the smallest boats, the *Riverside.* I was towing chemical products with the maximum limit, four or five barges on the Gulf Intercoastal. Clearly I was doing it just fine, so they couldn't say anything negative then. I learned not to respond to those "barefoot and pregnant" comments, too. If I just kept quiet, other guys on the radio who knew me would really take up for me. After twenty years of fighting for myself, I'd become established. Overall, it's a great bunch of guys out there and I enjoy working with them all. Pilots will give you the shirts off their backs.

There's only about a dozen women piloting boats today. It's hard because you have to put in time on the deck before you can get a license. There you might be, the only woman on board for thirty days straight.

Towboats can't turn on a dime. If you're on a pleasure boat and your engine dies when you're in front of a towboat, that towboat can't stop. If you're in a small boat out in front of us, you'd better be able to row real fast, because we don't have brakes. When I was captain of the *President* in Davenport, the closest thing you could see from the pilothouse was four hundred feet out, a whole football field away. So I'd hear this "nnnt, nnnt," like a gnat flying around my head. It was a jet skier, circling the boat. I stationed a lookout for a few days to report his location back up to the pilothouse, but after a while I just couldn't justify it anymore. It's important to make people aware of the dangers. There should be some sort of license required for pleasure boaters to avoid this kind of thing.

One of the scariest things happened when I caught a rope in my propeller on the *Commodore* on the Mississippi. I lost steering and my engines. Luckily the wind blew the right way and took us over to the bank. Another time, I had a shaft break and drop onto the rudder on the *Mark Twain*. I lost my steerage and had to go down into the engine room. I didn't know whether to tell them all, "O.K., everybody, get your life jackets on and get ready to jump." Fortunately, another boat pulled up alongside to rescue us.

There were times I've misjudged going into the locks with barges. If you've got three barges across, that's 105 feet, and the lock is only 110 feet, so you've got only 2.5 feet of clearance on either side. It's pretty tight when the wind's blowing and you've got 1,000 feet of barges in front of you, too. Definitely you have to wait sometimes before locking through because of the conditions—wind, current. It's part of the pilot's knowledge. There's a calculated risk. If you slow down, you don't have the steerage, but you've got to slow down because you can't go into the lock chamber full ahead.

Of all the boats over the past twenty-five years, the *President* is my favorite. I grew up on that boat. She had her own sway. She'd get up steam and just shake, rattle, and roll. Back when she was steam-powered, she had her own pace. And the smell—it was steam. Even when she was converted to diesel, she was fun to operate. She was a big boat, but she could do anything. She was like a parent to me.

I'd started my own passenger boat business in Baton Rouge, but business was slow during the winter, so I volunteered with Mother Teresa's order, which had a house in Baton Rouge. Whenever she traveled in the U.S., I drove her around. She called me her "bodyguard." On her third visit, she suggested I look into a vocation as a Catholic sister. I saw an ad introducing me to the Sisters of St. Joseph of Medaille. Before that, I'd known something was missing in my life. I took my first vows in 2000 and within a month was working with the Seamen's Church Institute. God set it up this way, and it's been a perfect fit.

My ministry is to listen. It's hard work out here with thirty days straight on the job away from family. Visiting with the guys, they tell me they're worried about their wives and children, about what's going on at their houses. They miss funerals, graduations, birthdays, anniversaries, even the births of their own kids. They don't want to seem like wimps, so they won't talk to other guys about this, but they'll talk to me. They'll get it off their chests. They work safer because it's off their minds, and they can focus on their work.

A lot of these men have grown up on shrimp and oyster boats. Many learned the work from their fathers. They can make a really good living. Usually I'm the only woman on the boat because most of them don't have cooks anymore. There will be four to eight men and me. I walk a fine line. I'm one of the crew, but I'm also the pilot, and I'm also a nun. And I'm a woman.

I do trip work now. They call me for a three-to-seven-day trip, so I'll fly to St. Louis or Corpus Christi to meet the boat. As a result, sometimes I'm nun by day and captain by night. Just recently, for example, I was in Cincinnati. I worked with my community in meetings during the day. At night I got to play captain on the *Belle of Cincinnati*. It all goes together. My life as a pilot and my life as a religious sister are always together. I'm not one without the other. When I'm a pilot, I'm moving concrete or coal or salt from point A to point B. While I'm doing that, I'm also talking to my crew, to people on the radio, and I'm hopefully being the hands and feet of Jesus to these people. I don't separate the roles.

When I'm in the pilothouse, I feel great. I love the job. I can't help but steer a tow on a beautiful sunshine day or a full moon night, and think, "My God, I'm being paid to do this." I'm in my glory up there. It's so conducive to prayer. On the boat, I'd have twelve hours to myself up there, so I might pray for six hours. If a deckhand wants to come up and shoot the breeze with me, he listens first. If it's quiet, he knows I'm praying. Once he hears the radio go on, he knows, "O.K., I can go up and talk now."

It's a good life. Given my druthers any day, I'd be sitting between the sticks.

Sue-from-the-Slough: Sue Mueller

My parents built a house on the Mississippi at Massey Station the year I was born, 1947. I spent all my summers there until I was in high school. My dad, Don Mueller, was born upriver in a cabin, a true river rat. He bought the first piece of property that was sold here and put in the road. His first cottage was an old railroad car covered with brown shingles.

When I was ten, he built an addition on our cottage from cement blocks left over from his dairy.

We had steps going down the hill to the river. There was a big bridge plank across the marshy land, and that's where our dock was, right on the back slough. I don't remember any DNR or Corps restrictions; we pretty much did what we wanted then. Dad made a contraption with pulleys and wire that would transport you and the boats up and down the hill to the river. He was always coming up with inventions like this, so he was the sensation of the ridge. There's hardly anyone left from the old days down here now. That's why my coming back and buying the old cottage is important to me.

From June until August, I never wore shoes. My mother never knew where we were, and she didn't have to worry—or at least she didn't think she did. This whole ridge was full of children, a big gang of barefooted kids who'd run up and down the hill. Waterlogged from jumping off the docks, we paid attention to only one rule: you had to have your life jacket on.

My family had a bunch of little boats and skiffs, so I had my own, a little aluminum boat with a ten-horsepower motor. I was five. I went out every day and took my friends. We went up the slough to Nine-Mile Island and back again. Dad showed me how to change the shear pin because I always ran over wing dams. Run over a branch, go back and lift up the motor, change the shear pin, and I was on my way again.

I zipped across the main channel, too, going over to Frentress Lake and other back sloughs. I'd get in trouble. I wouldn't be able to get my boat going. The Coast Guard rescued me so often that they knew me. They towed me back, yelling out to dad on the dock, "Don, we got Sloughfoot Suzy here!" I was always getting into stump fields and wing dams. I didn't care. I was a kid, having fun, the kind I thought would go on forever.

The wharf bar, the "Wakazu Inn," was just up the ridge. Wakazu wasn't really an Indian name, but it was trying to sound Indian, you know, like "You walk-a-you into the bar." It was *the* joint, the tavern, with a screened-in porch where people sat around playing cards. Dad spent a good amount of time at the Wakazu. If I knew dad was there, I'd go in, and he'd buy me orange soda and a candy bar. He'd tell everyone, "This is Suzy, my little river rat."

Dad rigged up a surfboard for me. It was really crude, just a plank of plywood. This was before people were tubing or water skiing on the river. It had a rope and two holes. All the kids loved to ride the surfboard.

Our big summer sport as kids was "Let's go wait for a barge." We'd get behind them with their big rolling waves, so we could ride their wake. The big burly barge guys would yell at us, shaking their fists, cussing. I'm sure they were scared to death for us, but we were just dumb river kids. We'd be laughing as we got as close as we could. We learned this from other river kids, and later, we taught younger kids, too. We could've gotten sucked under. My brother once came home and admitted "I sunk my boat, Dad." It didn't go over well.

Crazy Mary had her own dock. Once a week, we'd go and untie her boat. One person would be up on the ridge by her house ready. Once the deed was done, that person would call out, "Mary, Mary, your boat is loose!" She'd come flying out of the house like a bat out of hell, her hands in the air, screaming, "What will I do? What will I DO?!" One of us would pop out of nowhere and tell her, "I'll rescue it for you, Mary." She'd be so grateful, and we'd be laughing into our hands. We'd bring it back. "Thanks, thanks so much, oh you good children!" It was probably the only time anyone called us "good." We had it down pat.

Dad was a fisherman. He didn't go out and sit with a pole. No, he'd run his trot lines and take me along. You know back there where Sunfish Lake is at the back of Massey Slough? That didn't used to be passable, too shallow. But dad decided that would make a nice fishing spot if only he could get into it, so he took dynamite and blew that area up until he had a nice fishing pond. People still go back in there and fish to this day. Now that he's dead, the DNR can't come after him, I guess. And I wouldn't advise anyone to do that sort of thing nowadays.

When I was older, it was party, party, party. My parents didn't know. After dad sold the cottage, I wanted so badly to be on the river that my girlfriends and I would stay on Nine-Mile Island for a few weeks at a time. Mom would drive us to the Massey dock with our gear. Ten of us would go out in my little runabout with two big tents. Mom brought food every day to the dock, and we'd boat in from the island to retrieve it.

I remember combing the beach for hours once to find my friend's engagement ring. We spent a whole day diving for the ring in the muddy Mississippi, and of course, we never found it. Sometimes boys would come down by night and we'd party. We sunk a boat one of those times, too. We woke up the next morning and it was gone.

We had our own rules: No makeup. No hair rollers (everyone used rollers back then). No bathing—you could dip into the river, but no bathing. We'd go across the channel to the Frentress Lake Marina for our cigarettes. That was our daily trip. One day we're in my little boat, and our friend Smitty had lipstick on. The bleached-blonde glamour girl also had a towel around her head like a turban, hiding rollers in her hair. She was getting ready for the night. We yelled at her as we threw her out of the boat.

Missy was real particular. She wore little white booties, even on the island, to bed every night. She wasn't really a river rat, but she wanted to be—at least that's what I think. We all gave her a very hard time about that. When we get together on the island next year for a reunion, I'll have white booties for everyone to wear in honor of Missy.

We'd tell ghost stories every night in the tent until we got scared. One day we're lying in the tents and I hear over the loudspeaker, "Watch out, Suzy, here comes Dad." He'd come by for a little inspection tour.

Years later, after I was married, we'd moved back to Dubuque. Our oldest was only a year old. Right away I had to have a boat. My husband had never been on the river and was nervous about it, but I was oblivious to how he might've felt. Everyone loves the river; everyone wants to be on the river, I thought. The draw from the river was so strong on me that I didn't realize that he might not feel the same way. First boat we got was a cute little houseboat.

We had a lot of friends who had boats and little kids. The women sat in lawn chairs on the sandbar smoking, crocheting and knitting, talking, and counting heads. We loved the river.

One summer, when my husband had time coming to him, we took an extended vacation on the river. Many of our friends worked at John Deere, which had a major layoff. We parked our boats on the island for a few weeks. I had a job as a waitress at Timmerman's Supper Club in East Dubuque and had to be to work at 6 a.m. Sam, one of the other men, also had to go to work at the same hour, so he'd take me across to land where our cars were. I'd be there with my waitress apron on riding across the river. After work at night, we'd roast hot dogs on open fires, tell stories to the kids, get them safely off to bed, and then party, party, party ourselves.

There were wild times when we woke up the next morning and didn't know where swimming suits were or how boats had gotten untied, but we were young and the river gave us all the enjoyment we needed. The kids loved being together, swimming in their underwear, running around the islands, floating on the river. There were probably ten years when we spent every weekend in the summer together.

Eventually, we got burned out. After that one summer, as we all headed back to land, we glared at one another and said, "Don't call me . . . not for a long time." Our kids were growing up. I went into nurse's training. It was time for us to leave that life behind, but not the river. I'd never leave that behind.

That we almost died on the houseboat necessitated our selling it. We were coming back from Cassville and Guttenberg visiting family and camping on the river. We hit a big storm above the lock and dam. My husband, Ed, denied that things were getting bad. My best friend, Queen, was there with the kids and us. It was our daughter Mimi's birthday. She kept saying, "How can this be happening to me on my eighth birthday?"

Ed kept saying, "We're fine, we're fine." We were going into waves, dipping in and out of the foam. Lightning was flashing all around us. Ed pretended nothing was happening. He probably had to do that to keep a grip and keep a cool head. Meanwhile, I wanted off that boat.

I'd get everyone all lined up on deck in their life jackets and say, "We're going to jump. We'll hold hands, count to three, and jump." Queenie was crying and the kids were scared. I was scared. But then, just as we were going to jump, lightning would hit or a wave would wash over us, and I'd yell, "Hit the deck."

The engine quit. The boat started going sideways down the river, shifting 180 degrees side to side. We'd tip to the starboard side, and we'd all slide across the deck. The kids were screaming except for our son Ted. He was only three, so he'd put his arm around Mimi to comfort her, "It will be alright Mimi." We had no radio, but the Coast Guard spotted us. I'll never forget how happy I was to see them. I never set foot on that boat again.

It didn't keep us off the river, though. We got another boat. We still see that old boat on the river. People keep houseboats going forever on the Mississippi. Over the years we've had more boats, but now I've come full circle. I'm back at Massey, and I've got a little flatboat and a pontoon.

When we first moved back to Massey, I found simple things that make me feel like I'm seven again. When I walk down that road, I smell my childhood in the oaks. When you're a kid, you don't sit and look at "the view." It's just part of your life. But my mind recorded it. When my brother Shorty visited, he and I ran up and down the hill trying to find the steps dad put in from the backyard down the hill to the shore.

I'd love my grandkids to love the river. I take the younger ones over to Nine-Mile to fish. I want them to have river memories.

I used to go to the river for the thrill as a kid. As a young married couple, honestly, we went out to party and to manage the stress of young parenthood. Now? It's peaceful. It's nature. It's getting away from the rest of the world or at least getting away with friends and family to a place that is more innocent, truer. I love staying out on the islands. I love to pick up shells and turn them over, watch the gulls and the herons. See a bald eagle, and that's a bonus.

The river is in my blood. It was in dad's blood. All I have to do is look out at that river and I get a feeling I get from nothing else. I can't explain it. I guess that's what being a river rat is. You can't stay away from it.

Cottage Pioneer: Anise Bonnet

Frentress Lake resort was a family operation. My parents managed the properties, and my sister and I helped out. There was a lot of cleaning to do and the days were busy. But later in the afternoon, the Curtis girls and I would take canoe rides. We didn't go to town often, maybe once a summer to see a movie, but for the most part, we stayed right on the river. On the Mississippi, we call a back slough with only one outlet to the main channel a "lake," so when I'm talking about the lake, I'm really talking about a back slough. A lot of folks don't understand that unless they're from around here.

At night, we'd build bonfires and we'd sing camp songs. We made our own fun. My rowboat, *Cupid,* had a little engine on the back. I wasn't allowed to go out on the main channel of the river, but there was plenty of lake for me to run that boat on. There were forty of us kids who'd run up and down among the cottages and on the lake. If there was an empty cottage, we'd play there. We had our own parades, too. Once dad rode a mule in it.

We'd put on one show each year. We'd pick bouquets of white flowers and deliver them to every cottage and invite people to the show. We made hula skirts and we'd sing and dance. People from the cottages would come and pay—not a lot, but we were glad even to get a few cents from them.

It's been good being a girl and woman on the Mississippi. There was work to be done, and no one made much of a deal whether I was a girl or boy when it came to doing it. This resort property came to me from my mother, who managed it before me. She got it from her mother and father—my grandparents. I promised her I'd keep it all as rentable property and not sell the cottages or the land.

When circumstances forced me into selling the cottages to the residents—that was hard. At least we still own the land. Keeps it from being ruined. My son manages most of it now. I still do the books. For eighty-one years, it's been the only way of life I've ever known.

My grandfather, Charlie Heller, used wood cut at the sawmill at the lower end of the slough to build cottages back in 1902. There was also a farm, so the family had both sources of income. His wife, Lizzie, did a lot of the work, too. They raised turkeys, chickens, and horses. People say Charlie was quite an energetic fellow. When you look at the photos of Lizzie, you can see she was the type who could keep up with him.

In those early years, people came to the lake by horse and buggy. That was back when cottages had pumps; there was no running water. The cottages were named things like "Dew Drop Inn," "Lake View," "Palmetto," and "Idle Hour."

They used to cut ice out of the lake to use for refrigeration. Just operating one of the saws took enormous muscle. There were ice houses down here, too. Within time, that industry ended, and ice was brought in by truck. I went with dad to deliver ice three times a week to the cottages.

We picked up the garbage from the cottages, too. Dad dug a big hole in the field, threw garbage in, and burned it. If there was anything good and tasty in there, we retrieved it and fed it to the pigs. We used up as much of everything as we could back then.

There was also a tavern down here, although my folks didn't operate it. It was separate from us. Men would be taken to the tavern by boats like the *Reddy Red*, and then they'd drink beer and play cards. Once when the Feds were raiding the tavern for gambling, the owners asked if they could put that slot machine up in my parent's bedroom. There was little me sitting up in their room playing the slots just like a regular riverboat gambler. I've heard some people say that Al Capone hung out in nearby East Dubuque, but I don't know anything about his being at Frentress Lake. I sure never saw him.

Opposite of those Al Capone rumors was the time when one of the churches from town asked for permission to use the lake for their services. Next thing I know, they're on the shore baptizing people in the river. They'd dunk a person down and under right out of sight. I'm not sure how clean souls get in such muddy water, though.

The floods of 1965 and 1993 kept some people up all night sandbagging and running the pumps. In '65, the water was so high, I was surprised it didn't wash away some of the cottages. People at the lower end of the lake couldn't even get out because the road was under water. The flood of '65 lasted so long that anything left in the cottages crumbled from being under water that many weeks.

In any of those bad years, like in '65 and 2001, people living down here hauled everything out of their houses and carted it up to the back road where the ground is higher. It looked like a neighborhood garage sale around, here except that none of it was for sale. We lost a few renters after '65. It was just more than people wanted to put up with. Later, we raised up some of the cottages, which helped keep them out of the flood most years.

One of my favorite days at Frentress Lake was when the *Silver Eagle* gambling boat first came in. The water was high that day, but even in low water, they dredged to keep it deep enough. My mother would've been thrilled to see that boat come in here. It was a beauty—all blue and white, coming around the curve at the cut to the main channel, bigger than anything I'd ever seen on the lake before. Frentress people got upset at first because it was so big, but it didn't really cause trouble.

The *Silver Eagle* owners wanted one of our cottage properties and offered me a big hunk of money for it, but I thought of our cottage residents. I feel a loyalty to them. I wasn't going to give the *Silver Eagle* one of those properties no matter how much money they offered. Besides, I knew that if they ever left (as they eventually did), we'd be stuck with the building and a big dock that we had no use for. Meanwhile we'd have moved out one of our own renters.

I met my husband down here when I was about fifteen. He worked for my father. I didn't care much for Oscar until years later, after he'd been in the service and returned. Then we dated, and the rest is history. He was a good man. Oscar and I ran the place together until he became paralyzed. Then I did it on my own until my sons started helping out.

The island that separates us from the main channel changed overnight after the lock and dam was built in the 1930s. One day there was a big wide pasture there on the land between the lake and the main channel where my family's cows and horses grazed. The lock and dam was opened, and the next day the pasture was gone. The government made us give up the piece of land that was left. When their contracts were up, the government even made some folks take their houses down over there. They could do whatever they wanted back then, but I guess there's laws against that sort of thing now.

Before the lock and dam, there were low-water years, too. You couldn't get a boat through parts of the lake because of the mud and sand. It was that shallow. Some even say you could drive right across the lake.

No one has ever called me a "river rat." If they know what's good for them, they'd better not. To me, a river rat is someone who lives on the river—but not an admirable sort, if you know what I mean. In all the decades I've been managing the resort property, we've only had to ask two people to leave, two people who just could not cooperate. Sure, kids mainly, teenagers, they get rowdy at the cottages, but all I ever had to do was visit and ask them to keep it quieter. Most people on the river are pretty good when it comes right down to it.

At least the lake hasn't changed that much. I can't imagine growing up anywhere else. Being on a backwater in early spring, the wildlife is much the same as it was back in 1917—pelicans, butterflies, herons. Everyone says it's a good place to raise kids, and that's true. People always said this was one of the prettiest places to live on the Upper Mississippi. I guess I'd have to agree with them.

Brine

Child of Lake Michigan's western shore, where the tide's pulse is as predictable as breathing, I'm fascinated by wilder waters. Living now on the shores of the Mississippi, I take perverse, if sometimes astonishing delight, in the unpredictability and power of the river. Small wonder that Utah's Great Salt Lake, with its sharp rises and falls, has haunted me for years.

Down on the levee at the Dive In on the Mississippi early one spring, several of us gather to wager how high the river will rise. I find an article in a leftover issue of the *Des Moines Register* chronicling the Salt Lake's fluctuations, and I imagine it expanding and contracting like one's body in a fun-house mirror. It's too late for me to get to Utah in time to witness it, but the very next spring, as they close the Mississippi floodwall gates in town, I wait at the marina while Arnie replaces our prop and hear National Public Radio predict that this year the lake's sudden rise, by up to ten feet, will spill, claiming hundreds of miles.

My friend, a convert to Mormonism, tells me that in his Saints congregation in Virginia they pray about what the lake might do. In *Refuge,* I've read Terry Tempest Williams's account tying the lake's fluctuations to her family's fluctuations and her mother's death. Even professional journals and the *National Geographic* seem awash with startling tidbits—like how the salt content, roughly eight times that of the Atlantic, burns off moisture into evaporation in even the mildest summer heat.

Like Big Mama Mississippi, the lake seems to go its own way no matter how many times people try to harness it in.

By the time I am invited to give a presentation about teaching writing at a conference in Logan, just a few miles from Salt Lake, I have as much chance of turning down the lake as Ulysses did of resisting the Sirens. Flying miles above the water on the approach to the airport, I see the lake appear placid, smooth. It's the mirror of a quiet, lazy afternoon where I might lounge at its edge in a chaise and wear a floppy straw hat while I dig my toes in the sand and sip from a glass with a tiny umbrella in it. Babylon waters, pool of safety, a pond for healing—it seems nothing like the fierce, churning white water I'd imagined. Not my Siren, perhaps, but only some dogfish mistaken for a mermaid.

Not until later, when I drive out beyond the city, do I feel the familiar danger that those of us on the Mississippi know: *water rising*.

The lake emerges rather quietly for such a large body of water with an even larger reputation. Reaching the Saltair Drive exit on Interstate 80, I do not come upon it so much as it comes upon me. It reminds me of the mists rising out of the Mississippi River valley as the cool summer surface steam in the heat of sunrise. Just so, the lake comes gently, folding its diaphanous arms around my car. Within seconds, my whole world is lake.

Even before I turn into the parking lot, the lake greets me with its dicey perfume. Stronger than the aroma of small children who have been outdoors playing in July's heat, its briny fishiness recalls swamp sulfur, a rotten eggs assault, nature at its strongest. But the air here is far from hot. Despite the sun's glare that causes me to squint my way along the gravel path behind the Saltair public beach pavilion, I untie the sweatshirt around my waist and pull it over my arms to stave off the damp chill rising from the surface of the water. I'm told there are days when the heat sears salt into the skin, even into the eyes, but this is not one of them.

When it opened in the 1980s, this modern Saltair was hailed as a re-creation of the original Victorian beach building that stood on this site, a resort erected by the Mormons in 1893. The first Saltair burned to the ground in 1925. Turning the pages of the "History of Saltair" booklet chained to the desk inside the building, I find the Moorish architecture peculiar. Twelve pages of black-and-white photos reprinted from old magazines reveal the original Victorian structure, oddly fashioned like a Mediterranean mosque.

The pages depict pail-and-spade-toting, nineteenth-century beach-combers dressed in globular, striped swimming suits, standing in sun-pained attention for the photographer. Some waddle with rubber inner tubes girdling their middles, apparently unconvinced that the famed salt-buoyant waters would hold them up. I'm fascinated by the photos of the cavernous beach house with its carefully turned, mosque-like domes that seem to me authentically reconstructed but inauthenticity plopped right in the middle of the American West; they are as out of place as Dorothy's Kansas hot air balloon in Munchkinland.

The original 1893 Saltair was to be "a wholesome place of recreation," according to the Mormon ideal, enlarging Brigham Young's "This is the place!" founding declaration about the Utah territory he had chosen for his people. Abraham Cannon, an apostle at the time of the first Saltair's construction, admitted that the church hoped the place would become a "Coney Island of the West," thus sealing Mormon intentions of becoming part of the American mainstream.

Roller coasters, a Ferris wheel, bullfights, and vaudeville song-and-dance acts all performed on these resort grounds on the shores of the Great Salt Lake. But it was the body of water that galvanized people's attention. After the initial Saltair burned to the ground in 1925, it was reconstructed only to suffer the Great Depression and then another fire, high water, and fire yet again. But it was always the lake, not the pavilion, which drew tourists back.

We see the same phenomenon on the Mississippi. It isn't the Dive In or the charming bed-and-breakfasts that attract people summer after summer—it's the river itself. The river invites you to put a toe into its layered waters, and you do—no matter how quickly that toe might disappear from sight in the muddy flow. People gather by the hundreds at Nine-Mile Island and at Finley's Landing just to look. They come especially in high water when the river flows ominously full of creosoted railroad ties, Minnesota silt, and dead animals. Even in the middle of a hard January freeze, they drive to Eagle Point Park for eagle watches as the great birds fly overhead and swoop down to catch fish churned up by water and ice flowing over the roller gates at lock and dam #11.

Before Saltair opened its doors in the twentieth century, the lake had risen from 4203.25 feet to 4211.85 feet. An eight-foot rise might not seem like a lot—back along the Mississippi, we wouldn't even close the floodwall gates, much less sandbag, for that amount. But this lake laps a shore nearly as low and flat as the surface of the water itself. Even a slight rise extends the water's reach considerably. The ten-foot rise predicted would have caused the lake to claim an additional 240 miles of shoreline.

In 1983, banners proclaiming the restored resort's opening melted into soggy shrouds as high waters closed it down only months later. To the natural world, it didn't really matter. Humans might re-create their recreations a dozen times, but nature always has the last word. There is no turning back the natural clock—not on the cleverest imitation of an imitation Moslem resort, and certainly not on the Great Salt Lake or on the Mississippi.

Despite sandbagging, despite jetties built of railroad ties, despite the prayers of every Mormon in Utah, the lake submerged Saltair in its all-time high waters in 1984. Just nine years later, when we were having one of the worst floods of the twentieth century along the upper Mississippi, the salty waters of the lake receded. As we river-weary warriors were sandbagging homes and applying for federal aid, Salt Lake and Saltair negotiated an uneasy peace.

Drying brine had etched crusty lines along the interior walls at the two-foot and five-foot levels inside Saltair. Seeing these, I imagined them as inverted twin lassos drawn taut as a rope around a horse's neck, to hold him. I was almost sure the lake meant to leave no doubt as to who held the ends of those reins. Even though it slackens its hold during low-water years, without warning the Great Salt Lake will yank its briny lariat, choking whatever or whomever is in the noose; it means to keep everything it claims.

Nor is our Mississippi any more forgiving. Houses on the floodplain have similar lines where water, silt, and mud have risen in previous springs. Some owners have worked at having those memory lines pressure-sprayed or painted out of mind. Later, I will hear that the lasso lines at Saltair have been similarly painted out. Yet I wonder about such efforts to erase nature, to control even our recollection of its force. Water may recede, but the evanescence of the dangers of both the lake and the river issues warning.

For now, I am both delighted and terrified to be here with predictions in the air of another sudden rise. Those who would control the lake turn their attention outside to the shore. I watch conservation workers mounted on their backhoes, working on the beach. They are forming massive granite boulders into lines jutting out from the shore, underpinnings for the planks and beams that will cover to form piers. I get two feet closer than I think is reasonable and ask one of the men what the dike is for.

"Lake's gonna rise." He looks at me as if I am a simpleton. He is wearing a fluorescent orange vest.

"Do you think it will work?"

Now he is grinning. He's a big, Nordic type, with red-blond hair going to pale gray and light blue eyes. "This lake is one tough mama," he says.

"But do you think it will work? The jetties I mean?"

He's taking the opportunity to fish out a cigarette and light it. I doubt if this is an employer-permitted practice and want to remind him not to throw his matchstick on the white sand, but I am not that lake-crazed.

He says, "I been working on this beach for thirty years. One of these Ingineers always says 'put in a pier,' 'blast out a jetty,' 'put in some rocks.' I do what they tell me. But—no, it won't work. No matter what they call her—Lake Bonneville, inland sea, or a big tub a' salt, this lady is gonna do what she wants." He blows some smoke that heads immediately out over the water. "Keeps me employed. Lake and me both," he laughs.

Coconspirators, at least in my mind, he and I look over to where his cigarette smoke has drifted. I am sure that like me he is thinking about the lake's wildness, its persistence in resisting the lace doily attempts of those who would tame it, of those who would try to reconstruct the lake according to their own needs. I would like to talk with him about how the mighty Mississippi, south of St. Louis, has been forced into a canal-like passageway through hundreds of miles of levees that has no part of the Mississippi soul; I long to discuss with him my secret visions of a meandering powerful river sans floodwalls, levees, and locks and dams, but I don't. For the moment, I'm content to know that this Great Salt Lake will not be caught again in some Victorian restoration.

I leave the men to their work and take a short stroll, barefoot in the icy water, feeling sharp rocks cut into my heel. I suck in the briny air, nearly gagging. The rocks at the bottom of the Mississippi are rounded, slick, kinder. And not even the smell of dead catfish can compete with this salt air blast. Still, I am happy to be here, and happy to see that even on this cloudy day, there are others besides the workers and me who have braved the clammy air to come and experience the lake.

This is not a beach for the faint of heart or the faintly dressed. No bikini or scanty muscle shirt is being shown off today. One beach walker, skipping rocks and digging at shells with her boot-clad toes, pulls her thick woolen coat closer, reties her plaid scarf, and hunkers into the wind rising off the lake. Children bundled against this June day, too, walk the thick, cumbersome strides of winter. Having visited Florida's balmy shores just a month earlier, I can't help wondering—why do these people come here? What is the draw?

Why do I come here?

It's easy to see the attraction of Delaware and Maryland beaches in summer, with their quaint boardwalk shops and inviting shores. And, cuddled blue between the hills of Utah, Bear Lake, fifty miles northeast of here, gets its share of summer seekers with its calm, transparent waters that seamlessly join it to its river. I think of the more exotic places—St. Maarten, with its breezes that brush my hair as if it were prairie grass, or the North Sea, which rolls slaty and deep along the golf course in St. Andrew. In those places, I am invited to remove my socks and sandals and wade or even run in a free-as-the-wind canter.

Bending, I feel under the water for one of the sharp little rocks that has been piercing my feet and toss it over the rippling salt waves, thinking of one or two other places where the sea was so warm and clear that I was able to spot a freckle on my toe through four feet of water. Why, I wonder, come to places like this one, with its chill rocky sands that rake the heels and air that attacks the senses? Why this lake, where violent gusts blow out of the mountains beyond the Toole Valley bursting into twisters challenging even the most experienced mariner to a duel?

On the jagged shores of the Maine coast, I've had to hold onto my small son's hand to make sure he doesn't go over the edge. In western mountains, where I have camped with my family, I grew worried in the midst of summer about the very real possibilities of frostbite and the attack of grizzlies. So in midchannel on the Upper Mississippi River, where snakes abound, where undertows could drag even the strongest to the bottom, why do some swimmers insist on going the distance? What lures us to these untamed spaces? We go to these places, knowing these are the conditions?

We seek them out *because* they are chancy.

It seems to me we work so arduously to tame nature's wild places but then revel in its resistance. Primitive campsites are the first to fill in national parks. We backpack into the wilderness and up through the Canadian boundary waters with little more than a tin cup, a pack of matches, and a walking stick topped with bells to save ourselves from thirst, from freezing, from black bears. To carry more—foam sleeping pads, lanterns, a butane cookstove, coolers for meat and beer—anything more than wood, a jackknife, and a mackinaw? Any backwoods camper looks down her lean-to at such heavy packing. We herald most those who carry in the least.

Are we just creatures of self-destruction and contradiction, or is there something more here to explore? I wonder as I dig at a mussel shell on the beach with a branch of gnarled driftwood.

I walk back on the beach toward the parking lot, but then I turn to the water again, unable to let go just yet. It seems to me there is an answer here, and it is all braided into who I am and why I care so deeply for my cranky, problematic Mississippi River and for the other still-wild places of the world. Maybe the best clue is in how we match ourselves against nature even in our recreational sport. What is skydiving but overcoming gravity? What is ice-skating or water-skiing but walking on water? What is shooting the curl but a leg-wrestle with the waves? Although we enjoy the crest of the surf and the rush of air, it is only when we dip, it is only the fall that seals the experience.

Rock climbing against jagged limestone cliff faces using footholds that give way with the merest misplacement of a heel, we fight nature for the summit, a symbolic position of dominance even in lovemaking; yet we find ourselves enthralled by the stories of those it overcomes, those who lose their foothold, those who die up there. Unless Icarus plunges into the sea, we are not interested. We don't want him to die, but we want the thrill of thinking he might. Those who come to watch hold their breath not for the match, but for the climax where nature pins us to the mat and we have to give.

In the distance over Salt Lake, right now there are clouds that hang like parasails. When I watch those who parasail off the shores back on the Mississippi River—those who dare the land, the river, and the skies all in one sport—I see all of nature's seduction to wildness in a single, slow-motion moment. I have watched as boaters measure the length of rope extending from the back of the runabout to the parasail's crossbar making sure this umbilicus is long enough for freedom but not long enough to invite death by tree limbs or limestone bluffs. They strap the harness and check the buckles around the sailor who at the same time will be runner, flyer, swimmer, goddess. They wish her "Good ride!" and then leave her alone on the beach as they board the boat and slowly putt out into the river until the rope pulls taut. She thumbs-up signals for them to "Hit it."

Once, while watching, I heard the spotter yell that the line was twisted and saw the pilot's hand reach to throttle back, but it was too late to stop the sailor from being dragged to her knees before the sail, strapped to her back like wings, took the breeze and lifted her. I held my breath as her sail held the wind. Even once she was up, having cleared the trees and the limestone bluffs, I knew I was only waiting. As luminous and graceful as she appeared in the late afternoon sky, flying alongside herons and gulls, what kept my attention was whether she'd make it safely back to earth. Or would she crash into the rolling, unyielding current?

So we choose this entertainment, this sport, this risking of our lives. We visit easier activities on gentler shores at times, but we always return to the lure of danger, the lure of the wild. We feel the necessity to taunt nature in order to make sure that there is yet something in the universe more powerful than we are.

Ready now, I hold my hand up to shade my eyes under the glare that bounces off the water and take a long, last look at the broad expanse of this starkly beautiful lake. I am imprinting its color and jagged horizon, even its pungent air, on my brain. It will become part of me; I will take it back to the river I love and know them both better for the contrast they offer. This lake is becoming yet another piece of my wilder self.

Waving goodbye to the orange-vested workman who shared my moment of wishing the worst for human attempts to harness the Great Salt Lake (although I suppose he didn't actually know I was doing that), I return to the parking lot and get into my car. The high water is not here yet after all, so the others and I will not witness another invigorating human skirmish with wildness today.

Driving toward the exit lane of the lot, I glance over at another driver coming my way, a woman just entering this place. She and I acknowledge one another with a smile. I recognize her look, though. I've seen it on my own face when a big storm that's been promised doesn't materialize. It's all in the relaxed grin of relief you see trying to hold its own under the deep disappointment in the eyes.

Sometimes, when warned to evacuate floodplains and shores against rising water, my fellow river friends instead store up enough groceries to last a week, disconnect electricity, and haul the dingy up to the back door, so they'll be able to boat to the car on higher ground and travel on to school and work. They seem incapable of pulling themselves away from the perils of the spring rise. Where my mother lives along the Florida coast, she reports that some "crazy people" refuse to evacuate, preferring to stand out on the balcony toasting the advancing hurricane with raised margaritas. It is as though we need to witness wildness renewing itself in the moment when nature flexes her most dreadful power.

For me today, the experience of visiting this lake in the calm between rises and the inevitable reclamation of Saltair, has been more than simply watching a wild thing triumph over some silly conceit of civilization. Being here leads me to question—do we try to civilize the spaces and the creatures outside ourselves in order to tame those within? If human intervention and concrete could shush these wild bodies of water, I worry, how much hope is there for the survival of my own coyote howl? I have come here wanting to see some part of myself, or what I hope is yet a part of myself, affirmed. Unique and solitary, the Great Salt Lake, like the Mississippi River, has managed to hold its own against the inroads of humankind's ultimately baseless supremacy.

When conservationists seek to manipulate the existing freedoms of this lake, or when developers seek to take advantage of its pristine wealth, it seems to me that, in truth, all of us will only be better off if they fail. Only if they fail will hope still rise, spilling the banks of human containment. If there is nothing beyond human control, nothing which our technology, governments, and muscle cannot fix, then there is only one choice left to each of us. We must assume responsibility for it all. We must become god.

But when the Great Salt Lake and the Mississippi are no longer corseted by scientifically engineered shores and are left to their swooningly offensive fish smell, muddy bottoms, and jagged personalities—only then can our own desert places flood with imagination. Only then may the waters of possibility submerge those of certainty.

With wild waters such as these, taming the quick rise and containing the flood might make things pleasant and mannerly so that one might entertain the lake and river at Sunday dinner with the relatives. But this would be to handcuff our own human thinking, our hoping, our possibility. In such waters, to succeed in controlling—to find a way to walk safely on the surface without fear or any hope of possible submersion—would be the greatest drowning of all.

Bump

"Scine-tists and mapmakers don't know squat!" he tells me, this man with tattooed eels crawling up his forearm and winding through the lime-green stern-wheeler etched on his bicep. He has better ways to navigate the Mississippi, and the riverboat on his arm chugs along the rough waves of his elbow wrinkles as he talks.

He tells me about a full-load tow, how it pushes fifteen barges, normally arranged three wide and five deep. Once in a while you'll see seventeen, but it's pretty rare. Even at fifteen, the fleet has to be broken into two sets of nine and six in order to lock through. Bump, who is one of the pilots driving barges here for Clemens Marine, tells me that any more than fifteen is a waste of effort, "not 'ficient," he says.

I don't know why they call him Bump—maybe it has something to do with his generous beer belly that hangs and bumps fulsomely over the rail on the towboat when he meets me when I board; maybe it's his brusque way, bumping along the smooth manners of the well-to-do; or maybe it's a reference to how he steered barges when he first piloted the river. Whatever the etymology, I cannot imagine him with any other name.

Bump tells me that when the tows are moving up- or downriver late at night, pilots purposely shine their searchlights on the islands to see if they can catch any campers in a state of disrobement. "You'd be surprised," he tells me, "I get lucky pretty often." But even if all are quiet and clothed, Bump has a fine time waking everyone sleeping on the islands with his beams of light.

Bump tells me about steering the lead barge straight for the tip of Minnow Island until the slice in the hill gives way to expose two

The towboat *Valda* works its way downstream.

Barges awaiting cargo at Dubuque.

hills just south of Riverview. Then he knows he has to cut hard to the starboard or run into "one of them infernal wing dams, damn things." Like a lot of people who work or play on this river, Bump knows that those wing dams—and all the other reengineerings of the Mississippi—are what keep the river open for traffic. But like the rest of us, he doesn't have to like it.

Most of the barges on the upper river carry coal, gravel, grain, chemicals, and petroleum products. We quiz our eight-year-old: "Andrew, the barge ahead—empty or full?" In early spring, he stares down hard on the barge hulls to check for the four-foot section that rises out of the water, the empty hold exposed above the surface. By mid-June he's an ol' river rat, an expert spotting only the curved top of the barges cutting the surface and sings out, "full barge ahead" even before we hit the main channel. He steers straight for the point of Snake Island until cutting hard to the left just feet from shore to avoid the snag he learned about the hard way—bent prop last August.

We teach him, too, to respect the power of barges coming down. "Give us plenty of berth," Bump teaches me the day I ride with him, "it's pretty damn impossible to steer her 'round those runabouts. Git some damn fool kid out on the river with too much speed and too much beer in him and he's chopped tadpole before he rounds the bend." But he allows it's okay for the rest of us to share the river as long as we don't go playing around trying to cut his wake.

"Long nights," Bump says, telling me how some of the deck-hands pass the time casting off the side of the barge while they wait to lock through. "Mostly bottom-feeders, walleyes and catfish is what you catch by the dam," he scoffs. "Unless it's fish fry Friday, we throw 'em back in and they just float—bobbing, grinning at us, and then swim off down Dead Man's Slough."

Tonight I think about Bump waiting to lock through with his full-barge load. I think of Andrew learning the river, its snags and back-waters and where the water lilies grow, providing cover for herons. I think of them both reading the river for cuts in the limestone bluffs and watching the surface of the water for a break in the way the waves move, signaling an underwater wing dam. I think of Bump searching the islands for nudes. There may be a better way to live than having such sure signs to steer your course by, but I can't imagine it.

Sho-Gunning the Mississippi

When the "Star Spangled Banner" plays, Abraham Lincoln stands up and speaks, "Hachi-ju nen mae." Although Abe speaks in Japanese—quite a stretch for a nineteenth-century Illinois farmboy—Lydia, the translator, assures us it is the Gettysburg Address. As Lincoln finishes, "Okyakusama, moshi yoroshikattara, gifuto shopu e okoshi kudasai," I strain to hear something that approximates "shall not perish from the earth." Lydia informs me, however, that Honest Abe is inviting us to patronize the gift shop and sample authentic beef jerky. I can't help but imagine Buddha rising from a lotus position. He speaks softly in English, "Ladies and gentlemen, drop in at the Country Bear Jamboree and have a root beer float!"

The five-foot animated replica of Washington, D.C.'s Lincoln Memorial is the opening exhibit to American Village, a theme park three hours from Tokyo. While touring us through the village, "mayor" Mr. Saduki smiles repeating, "Wait until you see Mount Rushmore!" And sure enough, there is a one-half-scale replica of the presidents from South Dakota in the gardens outside. A full-scale replica of George Washington's nose is on display in the park restaurant so visitors can get a closer look.

I am part of a museum crew hired to design and install a Great River Road exhibit called "Mississippi River Country." My husband, Jerry, created and directs the exhibit. Wayne and Mark are crucial parts of the team both as designers and installers. As a writer, my job is to work with Lydia as she translates into Japanese our exhibit text about the Mississippi and about the ten states along its shores. This is our first glimpse of the exhibit being built according to the plans sent several months ago, and it is disconcerting; in American

Village, buffalo roam both the plains and the Rockies right alongside the *River Belle* pilothouse exhibits. As a museum director and the crew's historian, Jerry tries to explain to our host employers that they have both time periods and location mistaken, but Mr. Saduki likes the buffalo. They stay.

Our first concern is to track down artifacts shipped by the Midwest Express Company weeks ago, which are probably held up in customs. Fortunately, Saduki never bought Elvis's guitar for the exhibit. Although Elvis grew up in the heart of the Delta—Tupelo, Mississippi—and cut his first record just miles from the river, Jerry advised that it may inaccurately represent the Mississippi River valley to place Elvis's terribly expensive guitar next to a 29¢ copy of William Faulkner's *The Sound and the Fury.* This time, authenticity won. The guitar was out and Faulkner was in (although I wonder if the $250,000 price tag on the guitar had more to do with Saduki's decision than any allegiance to accuracy).

June 25: We work long days installing the exhibit. Although the crew of Japanese carpenters, electricians, and artists seem confused by Jerry and me working alongside them in the hall, they are gracious, and I learn a great deal more about Japan than I could have as a tourist. We've been relying heavily on Lydia, but tonight, as we work well past midnight, we find translation less and less necessary. At break time, toasting one another with ginseng tea, the carpenters share their rice burgers, and Jer and I pass around the Doritos. We compare our tools, holding up hammers and planes, most of them Japanese-made whether from the States or Japan. We compare our paper currency and mimic the faces of our countries' heroes printed on the front of bills.

Fukiyuki, master carpenter, seems startled to find me hammering next to him instead of another Japanese coworker, or an American man. I conjure up all sorts of cultural notions of gender inequality regarding what he must be thinking about me until he finally speaks, and I have to face my own stereotypes.

After working wordlessly for over an hour, he finally asks, "Please have American dollah?" He points to a photograph of a handsome Asian boy of seven or eight, taken from his wallet. As he taps the photograph repeating, "One dollah, one dollah," I think of Andrew, our seven-year-old son back in Iowa. Recalling that I promised to

Japanese and American exhibit team.

Japanese replica of
Mount Rushmore
(note movie screen
at base).

bring home "foreign money," I know instantly what Fukiyuki wants. I hand him the dollar bill. He tries to give me the Japanese equivalent in yen. Although I tell him this isn't necessary, he keeps saying, "Yosun, yosun." A slang term for yen, I think to myself. "He wants to know if you have a son," Lydia calls from across the room. From my wallet, I pull out the photograph of Andrew, and Fukiyuki gives me the Japanese bill. "Yosun... you son... your son... for your son," my ears finally catch up to his English. With the bison and the pilothouse behind us, we stand together in the dim exhibit hall holding hammers—and photos of boys an ocean apart.

June 30: With only a week before the exhibit opens, tensions rise, yet there is never a harsh word spoken on the job. Jerry explains that the Styrofoam catfish must be positioned within the traps, and Japanese overseer Mirimoto-san nods, yes, yes, and bows. There are smiles and agreement all around. But when workers install the catfish, they appear *outside* the traps swimming blithely through space. Disagreement comes through action, we learn, not through conversation and never through direct confrontation.

We learn to smile through the numerous photographs of Dolly Parton and Elvis being selected over those of Ella Fitzgerald, William Faulkner, Flannery O'Connor, and Louis Armstrong to represent the ten-state region of the Mississippi. They can't get enough of John Wayne, who (as far as we could research) never did a thing related to the Mississippi except to have lived in Winterset, Iowa—a town not even remotely close to the river. We smile, we nod, we agree when they say, "John Wayne, John Wayne, bang, bang." We plan on returning later to replace Wayne with Fitzgerald, O'Connor, Faulkner, and Satchmo.

They want *Field of Dreams,* so we have brought a uniform worn in games on the field where the movie was shot in Iowa. Just before closing the glass exhibit case and screwing in the bolts to safety-lock the uniform, I notice that the fly in the pants has not been zipped shut. I leave it in its natural state.

Before leaving Iowa, Jerry and I struggled with the text as we have done together so often before. We worked to get the language concrete, precise, and pithy. We consternated over parallel structure, metaphors, and cadence. Writing text for exhibit signage requires close attention to qualities of sound since it has to read aloud well; most museum visitors subvocalize or at least lip-read.

But now as Lydia and I work on translation, we struggle with far different concerns. Simple things that any American on the river would instantly recognize are foreign here. I explain in precise mechanical terms and gestures words like "wing dam," "barge," "lock and dam," "log rafts," "paddlewheel," "stern-wheeler," and even "steamboat." My own appreciation for the subtleties of the Japanese language also grows:

"We have two '-ing' words throwing off the cadence, Lydia. How will that translate?"

"In Japanese, it makes no difference."

"The verb tense here is a little tricky," I tell her.

"This is not a concern in Japanese."

"These clauses, Lydia, they have a parallel structure. Will that translate?"

"In Japanese it makes no difference."

Raised in Mexico by Japanese parents, trilingual Lydia has an insightful grasp on the deeper nuances of language and meaning. I learn a great deal about both culture and linguistics through our work. Together we pare to the core and I feel as though we are compressing a twenty-volume encyclopedia into a single haiku poem.

July 1: As we walk by the rice paddies on our way to work this morning, Jerry and I agree. We will not argue with the Japanese anymore. It's their show; they're paying the bill, and it's their version of America that will go on exhibit. Besides, we are beginning to feel like ugly Americans who insist on iced Coke and that our voices be heard over all others.

Tak, our friend and the liaison for the project back in the States, tried to prepare us for this, "You have to understand that after World War II, the government sent people to America to learn the culture and bring it back to Japan. But when we brought it back, it did not stay American. We make it our own, we make it *Japanese* America."

The more I think about it, the more I wonder why I think *my* picture of the Mississippi River region is any truer than *their* picture. I claim accuracy because I live on the river. I claim authenticity because, after all, I am American. But how likely is it that I have an objective view of the land where I raise my children, the shore waters where I swim, write, crick-stomp, work, ski, write, canoe, and love?

The Japanese perspective, focusing on America's fascination with movie stars and twangy musicians, may represent us more accurately than I would like to believe. They crimp the hundreds of miles between the mountains of the West and the limestone bluffs of Iowa as tightly as a closed accordion. The Japanese do not understand the concern we have with placing the Rio Grande exhibit alongside lead mining and riverboats. But when I look at it from the island of Japan thousands of miles away, Americans and American history may seem quite like that of all Western peoples. No wonder Sam Cheng back home gets so upset when people mistake the curve of his eyes to be Japanese instead of Chinese.

July 3: It is early. Rice farmers are checking water levels in their fields. Rice plants need to steep constantly in five to six inches of water. Because this is the rainy season, farmers rarely turn on the spigots that flood their fields. Watching them unleash the water today reminds me of the flooding on the Mississippi last month and the woes of farmers trying to dry fields so corn wouldn't rot.

Before starting work, I tour another exhibit, "Western Town," near the other end of the park. The sign for "Langhorne Clemens Attorney Office" hangs over a saloon where Japanese-featured Dean Martin croons a Willie Nelson tune. Up the street is a church complete with spire and cross. An animated preacher, with a Bible in one hand and a cross in the other, speaks to rows of empty pews. Occasionally he beats his fist on a pulpit carved with a traditional mural of Jesus at the Last Supper. All seems rather correct until I notice that a Jewish menorah stands on a small table to the left of the preacher. I wonder if the Japanese designers were trying to give fair play to both religious traditions. Or did they simply confuse it all as one belief, that which they might call "not Buddha" or "not Shinto" (as much as Americans tend to confuse Buddhism with Shinto)? I wonder what the preacher is saying. Is he inviting visitors to snap a photo in front of the Last Supper? Is he suggesting they buy some Asahi beer at the kiosk across the square?

Here in the heart of Sho-gun territory, I also discover two Asian actors performing a shoot-out on the reconstructed streets of

"Deadwood." Their authentic six-shooters about to be drawn, they count off paces. They shout jibes at one another in Japanese punctuated by American expressions, "O.K., Pardner" and "This town ain't big 'nuff for both of us." It feels like the movie set of a bizarre John Ford production with John Wayne being dubbed in by Japanese voice-over.

At another saloon up the street, a mannequin speaks to us in orgasmic Japanese rhythms, her eyes half-closed. Heavily made up and blonde, she looks much like Marilyn Monroe, Dolly Parton, or any number of women I have come to call American geishas. I won't need to ask Lydia what she is saying.

July 4: Jerry and I have been working with the carpenters and electricians since 4 a.m. There were no raised eyebrows the first two days we worked in the exhibit hall. Jerry was directing things, telling American workers who had flown over ahead of us how to modify the pilothouse and how to arrange sandbags to look more authentic in the flood exhibit. They expected this of "The Museum Director," a man they saw similar in position to Mr. Saduki. Mr. Saduki, however, has no contact with the workers; he channels his approval and displeasure through Mirimoto-san. In Japan, it would be unseemly for a man of Saduki's class to speak directly to anyone who has a hammer in hand.

But when Jer took up the staple gun on the third day, driven to meet the deadline for opening, I heard them whispering. The day I showed up at work in shorts wielding a wrench and questioning both Jerry and the carpenter about the placement of the Kentucky Derby poster, the eyebrows arched. I presume they are more horrified by me than by him since even professional women in this part of Japan should be demur, but they are too polite to object. "You are American," Lydia tells me. "It excuses everything."

Although the exhibit opens in only two days, this day feels as breezy as a summer afternoon kayaking Menominee Slough. Maybe it's because it is the Fourth of July and the American workers are determined to feel festive. More likely, it is because Mr. Saduki and Mirimoto-san are away in Tokyo.

The sun is finally coming out, and Hank Williams Sr. has been singing "Your Cheating Heart." American country-western music is piped all day into every crevice of the theme park—Patsy Cline,

John Prine, Willie Nelson, Chet Atkins, and occasionally Garth Brooks. But today the CD is stuck and I hear the line about tears falling down like rain over and over (and over) again. No one seems to notice. Lydia laughs. She recognizes the repetition, but she is the only Japanese worker who does. We place bets with one another to see how long it will take others to notice.

We work mainly on the aquarium installation. Japanese workers have been instructed to fill tanks with fish from local rivers. Jerry tells them that saltwater catfish are different than Mississippi River catfish. Everyone smiles, bows, nods, and agrees, but when we return from afternoon break, mackerel and saltwater cats swim inside the aquarium labeled "Mississippi Catfish" chasing one another's tails. Familiar with tail-chasing, we bow, smile, and invite Fukiyuki and the others to join us in lighting sparklers brought to celebrate American Independence Day.

Showered by the radiance of sparklers after a too-long day, we leave the park ready to collapse into bed. But Hank Williams is wide awake on the loudspeaker, reminding us that sleep is not going to arrive, no matter how late the hour.

July 5: It's Saturday. I slip my own CD into the park player this morning. Japanese workers and tourists do not notice that Pink Floyd singing "Another Brick in the Wall" is not country-western. "It all sounds the same to them," Lydia joins in my conspiracy. Crazy, wailing American music.

July 6: "Mississippi River Country" opens today. In attendance are unusual representatives from the ten states that border the Mississippi River, all of them young, middle-class, and Euro-descended. They prefer not to be called "beauty queens" as the Japanese tend to label them. I see two U.S. government officials—men old enough to be my father, old enough to be the grandfathers of these young women—ogle them. I feel as though I've stepped into a high school boys' locker room, but instead of pimples, the "boys" have gray hair and spreading middles. I wonder about my own culture that so objectifies women.

Miss Minnesota, Miss Wisconsin, Miss Iowa, Miss Illinois, Miss Missouri, Miss Kentucky, Miss Tennessee, Miss Arkansas, Miss Mississippi, and Miss Louisiana. In the months ahead, they will travel thousands of miles and make hundreds of appearances, all vying for the coveted Miss America title. The Japanese refer to them as "the Misses." Hearing this, Jer and I laugh, imagining a balding, pot-bellied man sitting in his truck outside a hair salon "waitin' for the missus."

These young women are strikingly beautiful. They are also young enough to be my daughters. "Eeeooow, warm Coke," I hear one of them moan. "What *is* this?" another whines at lunch, picking through a dish of delicately sautéed eels and bowls of minted tofu as though they are dead gophers. In my attempts to make them feel less foreign, more at home, I ask them about their families, interests, and schooling.

Hearing their answers, I feel as though I've tuned in to the Miss America Pageant: "Hi, I'm Karen and I love skiing! I also design and make all my own clothes! And my favorite thing to do is spend my days volunteering to teach English and bioengineering at the recreation department in the inner city! Of course, what I *really* want is to be a wife and a mom!" Jerry and I ask one of them to refrain from feeding chewing gum to the wild monkeys in the hills behind the park. And then I remind myself that the Misses are young and life is long. Hopefully the years ahead will make them grow wiser.

At the big celebration dinner, with Lydia translating, we talk with Yokatu, the geisha assigned to entertain us. She plucks a shamisen and sings. She explains the arduous training of a geisha: She learns to prepare traditional Japanese food, to become cultured in the arts, to speak English, and to wrap the many layers of her geisha robes "just light." Her primary job is to serve as companion to well-educated, wealthy Japanese men. She may accompany them to business dinners, affairs of state, or other ceremonial rituals where an erudite partner is required. Yokatu is eighteen or nineteen, the same age as the Misses.

Our official Japanese guidebook tells us that geishas are an honorable part of Japanese tradition and that, although Westerners often mistake the role of the geisha to be sexual, "This is not the case. They are among the most cultured classes of Japan." In Yokatu's case, I think this is so. But later in the evening, after many rounds of Asahi and sake, I see the older geishas pinching the rear ends of

Dinner party Japanese style.

some of our male hosts and following them off to private rooms. I can't help but be reminded of those American government officials ogling the young American Misses.

Regardless of which country we call home, we all live in two worlds: the world we proclaim in guidebooks, which sails full steam ahead like stern-wheelers on the Mississippi's surface; and the world that runs underwater, full of wing dams and snaggy river bottoms.

As I fall asleep our last night in Japan, I see overlays like the transparent plastic pages of an old encyclopedia. Under "anatomy," the first plastic page reveals skeletal structure, the second the muscles, the third the heart and blood vessels. Layering this soft Asian night, page upon transparent page turns across my dreams. I find Dolly Parton riding a buffalo bareback alongside John Wayne singing "Your Cheating Heart." Government officials bow respectfully to young geishas while winking to one another. I hear Elvis playing the trombone as Dean Martin sings "Jailhouse Rock" and the Misses feed tofu to mountain monkeys. Fukiyuki asks for American dollars layered by Saduki riding a catfish into the gardens as Mount Rushmore's George recites the Gettysburg Address.

On the final layer, Jerry and I pilot a steamboat through the island of Japan, cutting across rice paddies and shrines. But our navigational charts of the Mississippi River valley break apart. The lines on the chart separating river from land, state from state, and the United States from Japan become chopsticks, which form into Japanese characters, Kanji, drifting and swirling in an ancient Asian scarf dance—graceful, strong, and never-ending.

Gloria in Excelsis Polka

"We been playing polka over at St. Joseph's for ten years now," he says, scratching his navel beneath a mustard-splattered T-shirt. "MISSISSIPPI RIVER RAT" in three-inch-high letters runs across his chest. "Name's Ferdinand, but you can just call me Ferd," he greets us the day we pull the *Aesculapia* houseboat into the dock. This is the last boat slip, and we feel lucky to get it. It's Labor Day weekend at Spruce Creek, and Ferd is ready to dance. "You can wear your shorts to church," his wife, Ethel, entices us. "Even if it is Catholic, it's the polka Mass. We don't get too dressed up. You don't have to be Catholic, either."

Friday night, Ferd and Ethel and their adult children, Joanie and Wayne, along with their friends Hank and Trudy, serenade the whole marina. They chug along on their party pontoon boat, winding in and out along the docks singing "In heaven there is no beer / That's why we drink it here." Ferd plays the accordion, Ethel the harmonica. "You got any singers over there? We're short a bass," he yells out as he floats by. Unfortunately, Jason, one of our bass-voiced sons, is off at law school studying torts and criminal justice in Washington, D.C. James, our other bass-voiced son, is off at college wasting his time studying math and singing classical opera selections. If only they knew.

As Ferd motions Wayne to steer closer to our boat, he shifts the lyrics, "You're from the city and that ain't pretty, you're not so hot, you stole our spot." We discovered at check-in that Ferd had been eagle-eyeing our slip the day before we arrived, coveting it for his adult children who were boating up from Sabula. "Ferd's too damn cheap to put down a ten-spot deposit to hold the boat slip," the park ranger told us. "He does it every year." We may have shown up and paid the slip fee, but Ferd figures he has squatter's rights.

Undoubtedly, Ferd will also be spending his energies this weekend on rehearsal, on making sure the church air conditioning is working, on selecting his fashion for the performance, and on locating that bass singer. I hope he'll find it in his heart to forgive us in time for the polka Mass. It's difficult to dance when the lead accordionist stares down at you as if you were a no-account bottom-feeder. Under those conditions, it's even harder to pray.

At midafternoon on Saturday, our son Andrew and his friend Ian, whom we borrowed for the weekend, are tubing the river behind the runabout out on the main channel with Andrew's dad, so I'm off duty. By now, I am sure, those boys are whooping up the entire shoreline and daring one another to stand up on the tube. I'm equally as sure that Jerry is at the wheel encouraging them to do so and reliving his own childhood days skateboarding behind cars. Teenage Elizabeth is so desperate to escape "the parentals" that she's gone to a neighbor's houseboat to assist in making a cake with a blue Jell-O pond on top. Surrounded by brothers, she misses the company of her older sister, Bekah, who recently married and moved to Chicago.

Houseboat camping has the five of us living in closer proximity than usual, so it's no wonder we've splintered off this afternoon. The *Aesculapia* has a back bedroom for Jerry and me, but the kids sack out on sofas and air mattresses in the one big room that by day serves as kitchen, living room, dining room, and pilothouse. Since we long ago "adopted" Ian into our family, he joins Andrew in pestering Beth as authentically as a real brother, and Beth delights in similarly joking around with both lads. It's a comfortable arrangement, and we're all glad that Ian's parents have loaned him to us for the weekend.

During the 1950s, houseboats and excursion boats were the most common watercraft built in the United States. Enjoying newfound leisure in Eisenhower's postwar America, boaters clamored for vessels that would allow them to take on the roles of hapless weekend wanderers, floating free.

Last night after Ferd finally ended his dockside concert, Jerry and I and the kids spent "family time" playing five-card stud. I drained

Houseboaters, ca. 1900.

National Mississippi River Museum and Aquarium, Dubuque, Iowa

Leisure boaters, ca. 1950.

National Mississippi River Museum and Aquarium, Dubuque, Iowa

every last cent from the teenagers. At least that's *my* version of who the real card shark in the family is. No one has to know that, as the poker fairy, I returned the winnings under their pillows as they slept later in the night.

Gambling is a longtime tradition on the Mississippi, dating back to riverboat gamblers and French fur traders. As the cocktail glasses got lower and the stakes got higher, so did the likelihood that the game would end with one player shooting another. Riverboat gambling is a big business these days, with boats like the *Diamond Jo Casino* and the *Miss Marquette* enticing patrons to try their hands at the slots, the roulette wheels, and the poker tables. As with any betting establishment, some people go the boat only occasionally for the lark of it. When riverboat gambling first returned to Iowa, strict limits were placed on patrons, so one could only lose so much. Eventually, the limits were removed, and now there is a minority of gamblers who lose the mortgage and grocery money weekly because they are unable to quit. There must be healthier ways for cities and states to bankroll street improvements and schools than via lotteries and casinos. I'd feel better if there was a poker fairy on board the betting boats.

Although the slips and campsites here at Spruce Creek near Bellevue are more spacious than most, we live in closer proximity to our neighbors than in town. You try not to eavesdrop, but by the time I dealt the final hand last night, we heard Ferd from inside the camper parked alongside his pontoon boat: "Ethel? Where's my polka tux? I can't find it anywhere." How is a polka tux different from the usual sort, we all wondered over in the *Aesculapia*. "I suppose it has an orange tie with *polka*-dots," Beth quipped. "Maybe it's got straps built into the shirt to attach to the accordion, "Andrew added. Ian, however, was sure that such a shirt would make one dance the polka uncontrollably and unable to stop. Given what I felt was an opening invitation, I pulled Jerry to the front deck with me and attempted to teach them how to polka. "We'd rather play cards," Beth laughed instead.

With panoramic windows on the front of our houseboat, we couldn't help but see what was going on over at Ferd's, too. For the next hour, boxes, pans, and sheaves of sheet music flew out of the camper windows as Ferd searched the place. Ethel seemed to be assisting as she threw blankets, a couple of books, and a Crock-Pot out the kitchen door. But when I saw her harmonica land in the grass outside their camper, I couldn't help but wonder if Ethel had finally had enough.

Ten years is a long time to put up with a man who insists that playing polka music at church on a holiday is next to godliness, if you ask me. She tied a boulder to the tux and drowned it—I just knew it. I expected him to turn up on our deck at any moment accusing me of stealing the thing ("just like you stole my slip"), but eventually either Ferd found it or he gave up, because things grew quieter next door. Only "Strike up the music," from "The Pennsylvania Polka" played in the background. Then again, I'm sure I've let my imagination run wild making up these motives for Ethel.

We spent more family time this morning as Andrew, Ian, and Elizabeth took turns reading *Huck Finn*, especially the parts about leaving school behind. Elizabeth read, "The Widow Douglas she took me for her son, and allowed she would sivilize me; but it was rough living in the house all the time . . . ; and so when I couldn't stand it no longer," she pauses at this part, nods at Andrew and Ian, and all three of them finish the sentence in unison, "I lit out." They look right at me. I suppose they believe that since I'm a teacher, Huck's and Tom's joy at running away from school will bother me. Little do they know that teachers, perhaps more than students, await Labor Day as one of the most relished parts of our profession.

Here in Iowa, we start school before Labor Day, so our new term began last week, and my college classes are in full swing. I'm a lifer. I love teaching, the invigoration of working with fresh young minds each year, and even the smell of old-fashioned chalk dust, but today I'm being lazy. It feels good sitting here on the front deck, breathing in the river and writing. If Huck can escape school by lamming out for the river, so can I. In town it might be unseemly for a mother of five and college professor to be sipping beer and writing away the afternoon, but this is the Mississippi. Out here no one gives it a second thought any more than they do zebra mussels on barge hulls.

If I were still a lake girl, I'd have jumped in the water by now. It's that hot. On Lake Michigan, I always knew where the rocks were, where the bottom dropped off, where the sandbars rose up. Big Foot, a granite boulder twenty feet offshore from my childhood lake house, was named for its shape. A big "toe" and three additional

Girls' day out, ca. 1900.
National Mississippi River Museum and Aquarium, Dubuque, Iowa

"toes" stood three feet above the surface during my entire growing-up years from toddlerhood through adolescence right into young adulthood. If I returned to Beach Road today, I'm sure Big Foot would *still* be there. You can memorize the dangers of a Great Lake. Except for those slow decade rises and the rare, sudden rise of a seiche, there aren't a lot of surprises.

But here on the Mississippi, if I jump off the boat, I never know minute to minute what my feet might land on—stumps and truck tires carried down from Minnesota during high water, an old lawn mower dumped in upstream by a couple of lads the night before, a dead muskrat or two. If Big Foot had been on the river instead of the Great Lake, it could have shown up this year with fallen arches and by next it may have been amputated altogether or grown another toe.

Last June I steered the Larson right up to the beach at Nine-Mile, cutting through sand as smoothly as a hot knife through butter. Dry conditions up in Red Wing changed all that. When I headed for the beach two weeks later, I heard the dooming grind against the hull—rocks, timbers, and probably a rusted Weber grill were down there ripping into the fiberglass. The river bottom had changed again. I revved the engine into reverse, but not before bending the prop shaft.

Older river rats tell me the best insurance policy on the Mississippi is to have an extra prop on board, since there's no avoiding such snags. Even if you know the river like the back of your hand, the hand keeps changing, a wart here, a laceration there, and veins popping out all over. But for this weekend, at least, even backwater sloughs are maintaining a decent depth, there's no high water from Minnesota flooding down, and only a soft breeze ruffles the towels drying on the rail of the houseboat front deck. Later, I may float out in a tube tethered to the bow, but for now, it's just this pad of paper and me.

Looking through the rail of the houseboat down into this river, all I see is my own face looking back at me. This is not a river for those Caribbean lovers who can settle for nothing less than transparent waters and smooth shorelines. The Mississippi is never the same river in any two days, in any two hours. Low water today—with the opening flick of the locks or the onslaught of rain up north—can rise to high water tomorrow, making islands disappear and causing sandy beach to turn to mud. People on the river are about as unpredictable.

But for today, the river is flowing placidly, nearly a satin ribbon of coffee except for the runabouts and tows churning it up occasionally. We'll keep the life jackets on Andrew and Ian all the same, although at eleven years of age, they don't think they need them. The first thing we learned when we started on the river was to mistrust it—always. All kinds of things get carried off in the currents: abandoned flatboats, propane tanks, fallen trees, life jackets, kids. Safety tubes even around swimming Labradors are a common sight on the main channel.

Back when I taught high school, summers never passed by without at least one of our students drowning in the river. Sometimes it was a boating accident; other times it was a kid who was rock climbing but missed a step and fell down the cliffs into the slough below. Once it was Charlie, who had just graduated. He and his friends were swinging from ropes and diving in just south of Menominee Slough. Charlie's turn came, he grabbed the knot in the rope, he swung wide out over the river atop the limestone cliff, and when he reached the height of the arc, he let go.

Did he wonder about how eagles feel soaring above the rocks? Did he laugh with the rush of hitting the surface, the river pushing the breath out of him? We never knew. They said Charlie hit his head on a rock at the bottom. These deaths are the hardest, the deaths of teenagers at the height of health, the deaths of exuberant Hucks loving the river with every last breath.

For the lack of a life jacket just this past spring, Boise Cranston died on the back side of Schumacher Island. Boise grew up on the river, knew the sloughs the same way you know your own stairs in the dark at night, feeling—rather than seeing—how high to raise your foot for the next step. Friends say Boise had gone to check the prop at the back of the boat. One minute he was there cussing at the Evinrude and the next he'd slipped beneath the surface.

The current probably took him to the bottom and down the back side of the slough, the Coast Guard guessed. Burial at sea—they never found his body. It happens every year. Even old river rats like Boise are claimed by the river. When I think of a fellow like Boise, I suppose he'd have thought there was no better way to go. "Wouldn't want to die with my boots on," I can just hear him saying. I lift my bottle of Dos Equis saluting him.

Just as I sip the beer, out of the corner of my eye I see Ferd's party pontoon rounding the docks. No more tunes about stealing slips, I groan internally. "We still hope you come to the polka Mass Sunday," Ferd informs me, "We forgive you for taking *our* slip." Ethel winks and hands me a warm six-pack of Budweiser from the deck of their boat. Ethel's manner already reminds me of Edith Bunker, so I understand her peace offering. But Ferd? I can't imagine what stirs his sudden change of heart. "By the way," he says, "your husband's a pretty big guy. Any chance he sings bass?" My East Coast city-born husband isn't about to sing with a polka band. "He's a tenor," I lie.

I swear it's getting hotter out here, even if it is past four. They say maybe rain late tonight will cool it off, but for now, I'll depend on the occasional breeze and a dip in the big river later. Shirley Connors stops by asking about the leak in the roof of the houseboat. I met her over at the gas dock this morning when she was pumping out, clearing the boat tanks of wastewater and sewerage. "You should try Melvin over at the Barge Inn Marina. He's got a solution for everything," Shirley advises. Knowing Melvin's prices, I plan on giving duct tape another try.

Whether to extend the locks on the upper river—that was the main topic of conversation at the pump station this morning. "Longer locks is just gonna be better for tows," Tommy preaches at us, "be able to push all the barges through at once instead of having to double lock. The tow won't be waiting out there past the gates burning up fuel waiting to take the second set of barges through." They get glossy-eyed talking about lock and dam #15, where there are actually two chambers, one double-long at 1,200 feet for barges and another, smaller one for pleasure craft. Helen joins Tommy on the soapbox, "Damn tree huggers. They want to kill this river is what they want to do. If the barge industry can't use it, it'll just dry up."

Although folks at the pump station appreciate the beauty of nature along the river, they don't always consider practical things like extended locks from the perspective of environmental consequences. I picture my river environmentalist friends back at the college wincing. How will extended locks affect wildlife along the river? How much increased traffic—swamping the shore, burning gas and oil—will extended locks invite? A whistleblower report about Corps of Engineers' cooking the books in order to make extended locks look like a financial and environmental panacea complicates the matter even more. Why cook the books if they're already done to perfection?

I appreciate how using the river for commerce means that even industry cares enough about the future of the Mississippi to keep it moving along. I often worry that in the United States, only that which makes money will attract money enough to preserve it. Will senators, congress members, and governors invest in something as necessary as the Mississippi only if there's constituent votes in it for them? The barge industry, like all commerce, is interested in increasing profits: How far can they go in making a buck before incurring environmental havoc, and ultimately biting the hand that feeds us all?

In my earliest years on the river, I worked arduously to remove all vestiges of human engineering. Remove the dams, I'd think to myself while joining other radicals holding signs protesting human channelizing of the Mississippi. Get the barges off this river, and let it return to its own corridors and own meandering, I naively hoped.

But then I had to face that this simply was not going to happen.

There's too much invested in a locked and dammed, levied and floodwalled waterway. Like dogs domesticated for generations, the river could not return to its wolf-and-coyote self even if given a chance, at least not at this point.

Too, I had to start asking myself how far environmentalists will go ignoring the inevitable: If goods aren't transported by river, then the burden will shift to the trucking industry and rails, neither of which boasts the best of records when it comes to air quality. One barge carries the load of sixty trucks, towboat captain Joy Manthey once reminded me. "It doesn't take a rocket scientist to figure out that one full fifteen-barge tow transports enough cargo to fill nine hundred trucks. We can't continue knocking down trees and building five-lane highways for trucks." If cargo shifted from river to land transportation, she's right; there would be numerous increases—all the fumes, all the busier highways with more accidents, all the concrete resulting in more runoff.

The longer I am on the river, the more I realize that environmentalism is far more complicated than my original nature-loving view. Land and air pollution and global warming enter into the conversation of the transportation of goods. Barges wreak less havoc on air quality than the trucking industry. Yet I've seen the devastating results of the engineered river south of St. Louis, where the once mighty Mississippi is now little more than a winding tight canal. On the Upper River, I've seen, too, the decrease in habitat and wildlife on these once wilder waters.

We Americans are hell-bent on more, more, more—more goods and a more luxurious lifestyle. We even fight senseless wars in order to preserve our way of life; witness our middle-class economy fueled by dependence on foreign oil. Best for the total environment would be to reduce our lust for cargo and our increasing tendency to redefine "want" as "need." But since I don't believe we are any more capable of doing that than are the barge lines of volunteering to reduce their profits, land versus river transportation seems doomed to a showdown. Will it be "One, if by land, two, if by sea"? Will we save the Mississippi if it means destroying land and air? Can we afford to do anything *but* save the Mississippi River?

For now I settle on the middle ground of maintenance of existing locks and dams without escalation. Although the normal course of

American engineering and development seems to strive for always going farther and hungers for bigger and more, this doesn't have to be the route we take on the Mississippi. To increase industrialization and channelization will inevitably result in the loss of yet more habitat and species. Don't blow up the dams, but don't extend the locks either. My greatest hope is that those with no axes to grind and no profit to gain study the complete environment with a realistic eye to predictions for cargo transportation needs.

A puff from the cottonwoods across the way floats down and settles on the tip of my nose, making me sneeze. These are serious thoughts and I'm beginning to kick myself for entertaining them at such length on such a beautiful afternoon. Besides, what we don't know about the environmental and ecological impact of channelizing and controlling the Mississippi makes me reel. Either that or it's this beer.

As I think about it now, sitting here on the deck, this perfectly wonderful deck, I suppose we boaters and fishers have no right to call the kettle black. We go running up the back sloughs where no barge would ever fit. Watch our wake pummel the shore, watch how it bends the reeds, how it swamps the water lilies, how it inevitably sends least terns and egrets running to the dunes. Wave runners and jet skiers? Don't get me started. But what's to be done? Turn the river back to presettlement days? No one would buy it. I don't want to move off the water, myself. Solutions to keeping this river alive are as muddy as the river.

I suppose Jerry and I, Beth, Andrew, and Ian will head out for the islands later and haul the boat up on the sand—or on rocks, whoever can predict? I'll probably cool off with a plunge just before dinner. Then Jerry and I will lie on our backs in the last of the sun-warmed sand and talk about how good life is. Beth, Andrew, and Ian will argue up on the dunes about whose driftwood fort is best and about how to build the bonfire for the night. And we will all resist the passing of these three days as surely as Ferd resents our stealing his slip.

But for this afternoon, I'm leaning back, my feet propped up on the railing, my eyes closed in the afternoon heat, rocking, rocking back, finding a river that moves beyond dream into real life. It is a real-life beautiful day and a real-life late afternoon sun that slants

Good cheer on the *Aescuplapia III*.

across the deck. Real boats are listing languidly in their slips. I sit here, empress of my own boat, my pen, my scepter. I toast the river with each sip. Here's to you, you wonderful, terrifying, raging, lulling river. And as I rock back in my deck chair, I hear Ferd playing the accordion in the distance as the polka Mass begins and the congregation sings "In Heaven There Is No Beer."

Fish Tales

Ten Lessons from Boating the Mississippi

After only ten years of boating the Mississippi, I am far from having full river-rat status. Yet I've learned enough to pass along the following tips with certainty. If they save only one toe or one prop from being the victim of the kinds of accidents I've foisted upon myself and others, it'll be worthwhile.

1. Never dangle a toe in the river.

You may not believe this, but what I'm about to tell you is true, and I can prove it. It's in the Iowa Department of Natural Resources crime files. Jake, the boyfriend of a young friend of mine, was lazing along the boat docks last summers. He's not a river person (as you will be able to tell from this story).

It was July. Jake was hot. He plunked a toe in the river like little Jack Horner sticking his thumb into a pie, but Jake didn't catch any plums. A big old stinky catfish came up to the surface, thought it saw a worm, took a bite, Jake yeeeee-owed, and pulled out his toe with the catfish on the end of it.

Jake was rushed to the emergency room. Once they fixed his toe, the DNR came in and slapped down a ticket. Jake went to court to protest the citation. The judge, who knew a landlubber when he saw one, acquitted the case faster than you can catch walleye downstream of a wing dam. His alleged infraction? "Fishing without a license."

2. Always have shoes on board the boat.

Underwater stump fields are not kind to bare feet; nor are rusted Volkswagens, hog entrails, catfish, and broken beer bottles. You never know when you might run aground and have to get out and push, lift, or dig.

3. Don't skinny-dip in the main channel.

If you're not wearing a swimming suit underneath your shorts and tank top (and you're female), wear matching underwear to pass as a swimming suit, at least from a distance. Don't plan on swimming au naturel when the spirit of the irresistible Mississippi moves you to dive in. The DNR doesn't take kindly to naked swimming. Besides, you never know who's got binoculars out there. Remember that Bump the barge driver is still out there on the river, spotlighting for nudes.

4. Never putt-putt an empty lake or slough.

You might think you've found the quiet hideaway stream, but if there's no other boats in the inlet pool, there's a reason; you've found a pond full of sawyers and shoal water. So unless you want to use those shoes (see #2), steer clear.

5. Give barges a wide berth.

Towboat pilots, skilled as they are, can't turn barges on the head of a dime. In high water, in fact, barges have a tendency to run away from their tows. There you are sitting out in the middle of the channel with a fifteen-barge tow churning your way, blowing its warning. You never know when your motor will quit or you'll lose an oar.

6. A straight line is *not* the shortest distance between two points.

Never attempt to cross what appears to be a straight line just beneath the water's surface. Not all wing dams are marked on the Corps of Engineers maps, but an experienced eye can see the straight line under water and recognize it as an underwater dam. Props and hulls are expensive.

7. The spring rise bears gifts.

Watch for skiffs, canoes, water skis, abandoned floats, or empty barrels (to bolster your dock), beach furniture—all free! At least until your neighbors upstream discover these things have run away from home and they come hunting. Watch out for dead hogs and cows. No one will come hunting to retrieve these.

8. Remember the iceberg.

For anything you see above the water, assume that 90 percent of it lies beneath the surface. Like those innocent willow branches with a few green leaves on them that show up on the river's surface after the spring rise recedes. Assume the whole tree is down there just waiting for your hull (see #2 and #4).

9. Don't go a-knockin' when the boat's a-rockin'.

No matter how close those friends of yours on the next house-boat are, if their boat is rocking and they're not visible, they don't want you to visit. Trust me on this one.

10. It's muddy water.

Visibility is usually less than twelve inches. Whatever falls in the river, stays in the river—keys, a wedding ring, cows, camera, your soul.

Catch and Release

Locating available residential property to buy along the Mississippi is like trying to find your way up a back slough at night—without lights. You have to nearly smell your way to it. You have to get desperate. Desperate enough to visit the local haberdasher so that as he fits your husband for a suit, you ask him, "Ever hear of river property coming up for sale down near your place on the river?" Desperate enough that you order pork fritters at the Massey Grill just so you can pump Carol for insider information, "Know of anyone selling a cottage on the river these days?" Desperate enough that even inland at the Mississippi Mug Bean and Brew House on Bluff Street, you interrogate each patron who walks through the door, "Haven't heard of any river houses coming on the market, have you?"

I have kept my ears to the waves for years—among pontooners and johnboaters at the docks, in the bait and boat shops, eavesdropping at gatherings of jet skiers over at Nine-Mile Island, and at polite cocktail parties in town where I ask discreet questions "for a friend of a friend." I feign avid interest in all the gossip of how Ms. So-and-so loves her cottage, how much Mr. So-and-so spent on raising up his place on stilts after the last flood, but only when talk turns to foreclosures and deaths do my ears turn like satellite dishes seeking the right signal.

Good residential property right on the river is so rare that it usually only becomes available through mortality or misfortune. Exceptional is the homeowner who simply decides to sell her river home, lists it with a realtor, and it appears right there over the coffee in the classifieds. More likely, someone's father or aunt dies, leaving the property to offspring. Occasionally, someone can't make the payments, the bank takes it back, and before you know it, over his auctioneer's hammer, Ken Mozena is chanting, "Now, ladies-and-gentlemen, we-have-a-fine-river-property, a-one-of-a-kind, from-the-front-room-you-can-see-Newt-Marine-*and*-the-main-channel: WhatamIbid?"

Call me a casket chaser, but I keep my eyes to the obituary pages for news of anyone dying along the river without heirs. Not wanting to uproot our children attending schools in Dubuque, my husband and I decide that river offerings at distant places like Têtes des Mortes, Bellevue, and Guttenberg are out of the question. As impossible as it is to get in at nearby Frentress and Shawondassee, we escalate our efforts to find a place there, since both are within an easy drive of town.

Skipping over the "Houses for Sale" ads, I scan for legal notices in the newspaper looking for foreclosures. I circle these in red and use the folded back page as my triptych on countless drives up and down the shore tracking down every listing.

I am without shame when it comes to interrogating the proprietors of my usual haunts. Stopping in at Rondinelli Music and Audio, I drop off our son's guitar for bridge work, but my real motive is to grill George about river property. Not a river rat himself, George Rondinelli has done business with most of Dubuque and East Dubuque through his work as an audio specialist for concerts, plays, live remotes, and the like. But he hasn't heard even a whisper of shoreline residence up for sale. Other errands find me pitching the same inquiry to Linda, the hair stylist at University Cut 'N Style. I leave the shop with less hair but not more leads. Rick-the-Post-Office-guy, a regular on Nine-Mile Island in summer, is only able to tell me how much it'll cost to mail out my *Dreaming the Mississippi* manuscript to publishers.

At other places, I end up anything but empty-handed. Visiting Martha at River Lights Books, I come away with yet another copy of *Huckleberry Finn;* at Outside the Lines Art gallery, Connie and Stormi sell me on a pair of silver and jade earrings; at Jamie's wine shop, my inquiries result in my carrying away a bottle of Sauvignon Blanc; the maître d' at the Captain Merry restaurant is able to help me with a reservation for dinner. Instead of riverine residence clues, I walk out of Fiber Wild with three skeins of Himalayan silk yarn.

And although the pharmacist at Hartig Drugs fills my prescription, she is unable to fill me in on places on the Mississippi. Miguel Sanchez brews a smooth cappuccino at his coffee bar, but when it comes to riverfront property, he draws a blank. Not even Ron from Vaughan's Mr. Muffler (who drops anchor nearly every summer weekend in one backwater or another) can offer the merest hint of possibility. As their *no*'s add up, so does my desperation to find a river place.

Jerry and I continue leaving business cards with numerous people. Hundreds. Three years of baiting the hook, and we finally get a nibble.

Our friends Sue and Edward reeled in their fish, a cinder-block house with a second, smaller cottage on the adjacent lot, north of town at Massey Station just below the Shawondassee ridge. The house was small, but the property was big, the potential for renovation immense, and most of all, the river view vast. That the hand of the cosmos was in it, I have no doubt. Notice of the auction appeared only as a tiny ad, and Sue just happened to recognize this as the house she'd grown up in. She and Ed had dreamed of other places—a resort along North Carolina's outer banks at Cape Hatteras, a Minnesota inn at Stillwater, an A-frame in Galena. Any one of these could be retirement, they said. But when the place she'd known as a child as Mosalem Manor came up for auction, Sue and Ed snapped it up as quickly as eagles plucking shad off the surface of the river.

They are handier than Jerry and I are, however. Faced with gutting the one-story cottage, installing trusses above to make upper bedrooms, and building two decks overlooking the river, our friends merely rolled up their sleeves and went to work. It took more than a year of constant labor. While Ed wired and plumbed, Sue sanded and varnished pine floors, plastered and painted every inch of wall, and planted out the yard. Together they rebuilt a dream home on the bluff over the backwaters of the river.

Jerry and I helped as we could, but let's face it: We're a couple who have spent our lives with our noses in books rather than with screwdrivers in hands. We are complete know-nothings in the world of practical things. The gift of opposable thumbs is only wasted on me. The only practical thing I know how to do with mine is smash them with a hammer.

Sue and Ed feel safe enough to let us help them clean up and haul away the yard art and basement relics left by the previous owner. What we learn during the conversations while helping them is that when you're fishing for a place on the river, you have to go about it quietly. Joe from the men's clothing store, who had become our good friend during the course of the hunt, warns us, "Send out the lines, yes, but if you get a nibble, keep it nice and steady, hold onto the rod, reel it in carefully, quietly, as quiet as the river at four o'clock on a Tuesday morning."

If word gets out that you've got one on the hook, radios blare, megaphones to the whole town turn on, "Kate has a live line over on the river!" Others rush in, and before you know it, you've lost your chance. The big one gets away or is carried off in the nets of another fisher.

There are three kinds of residential property in this region. The best, or at least what I would call the best, is so hard to come by that it's common practice to bid competitively on it. Sue and Ed's place at Massey Station and nearby homes at Shawondassee are sold through auction or word of mouth. Entrepreneurs like the Bonnets and Petitgouts own the choicest lots in the Frentress Lake region, those lowland enough to have direct access to the river but high enough (or on stilts high enough) to keep residences above flooding waters, at least most of the time. Their ancestors bought acres of property long ago and have passed it down through the generations. They lease individual lots to people who buy or build houses on them. You own the home, but not the turf underneath it.

At the turn of the century, lots at Shawondassee and Frentress were clustered into groups as river resorts where people from the big town of Dubuque spent a week or weekend escaping city heat by luxuriating in cool water and shady beaches. The original landowners ran the resorts, sometimes provided meals, and rented out cottages. Now as then, the river may flood into their homes in century-high years, but otherwise residents have a view unfettered by railroad cars.

With the resorts gone and the rented cottages now owned by individuals, however, many wonder why the Bonnets and Petitgouts persist in leasing rather than selling these lots. Do they really have plans for billion-dollar developments at some future date (as many along the river worry)? Are they merely concerned about the

Day-trippers to Frentress Lake Resort, ca. 1900.
Telegraph Herald, *Dubuque, Iowa*

environment of the riparian and river and thus keep it carefully proctored (as many of us hope)? Has it become as inextricable a part of their family heritage that to let it go would be tantamount to putting their elders in nursing homes before their time? Or are these simply cherished family holdings that they don't want to split up? No one knows for sure; possibly *they* don't even know for sure.

As risky as it sounds to buy a house when you could have the land pulled out from under you in any given year, there are those of us so thirsty to live in residences on the river in such places that we'd gladly drink down the conditions—mud, legal snafus, or having land yanked out from beneath you.

A second kind of river property sits lower on the floodplain, like at Shore Acres, Illinois. Houses there are easier to come by. You can buy a ramshackle place more easily and at a more modest price than at Massey or Frentress, but within ten years you'll get flooded five to seven times. Even if you keep an empty basement, hose off the mud, and repaint, what do flooding waters do to foundations? Pulleys attached to the ceiling of the living room are at-the-ready in some homes to hoist sofas as soon as a single drop seeps in. How often can one put up with sludging out the mud and bleaching out the mold in the aftermath?

These Shore Acre houses are the ones you see on the TV news floating down the main channel with hound dogs on the roof. In Noah years, you read these owners quoted in newspaper stories: "One too many times. We're moving out." They're desperate, too, but mostly they are as worn down by the river as is a stone sanded smooth in a waterfall. In the past, many residents would finally sell cheap just to get to higher ground even if it meant moving to a trailer court. In more recent times, however, with community support, Federal Emergency Management Agency (FEMA) has been buying them out.

Since railroads were often built parallel to flat riverbeds, those who live in these lowest areas usually also have the rails running between them and the Mississippi. If they don't wake out of a deep sleep to the sound of water lapping against the front door, they'll be shaken out of bed with every blow of a train whistle.

Then there's a third kind of river property. These houses are so high up the bluffs that the river is more a painting on their walls than a pulsing lifeway. You can *see* the Mississippi from there—the barges moving downriver in slow motion at that distance, the current breaking waves on wilder days; but you can't smell it, oily catfish or the mud of it; you can't hear it, the bass octave of towboat foghorns or the tiniest of hummingbirds twittering in the cottonwoods at the head of an island; you can't feel it, the thick wetness of a river that enters your pores, that floods your lungs whenever you inhale.

Neither as troublesome as the lower floodplain property nor as hard to snag as Frentress and Shawondassee residences, these immaculate homes are the frequent choice of the well-to-do. They come on the real estate market regularly but at a pretty penny. This remoteness, to say nothing of the forbidding cost, wouldn't do for us.

We stop at Carol's diner at Massey Station again for pork tenderloin. I eat the pork; Jer eats the mashed potatoes. Like a fisherman checking his catfish traps, he asks her, "Had any action on my business card for a river place?" Carol grins, wielding her spatula in the air like a symphonic maestro. "Gray-haired guy come down here from Shawondassee, had the Ham Supreme," she says. "I asked him, and he says, 'who wants to know?' So I give him that business card you left a few months ago." Carol pauses to squirt more grease on the grill and flip slices of tenderloin, "I told him that you were a nice enough fella," she continues pointing her spatula at Jerry and winking at me, "and that you've got a good wife who likes my pork tenderloin. He looked at the business card and laughed like a hyena. Said he knew you." But Carol can't remember his name. "I think it starts with an *H* or something."

Back at home, I leaf through our Rolodex of addresses, old Christmas cards, and photo albums of friends trying to discover who the mysterious *H* person might be. There's John Hinton, but he lives in the suburbs far from the river. Mame Hardy, I'd heard, moved to Florida and sold her river house over a year ago. I go through the cards a second and third time and still come up empty-handed. Two days later, Howard Higley calls: "Had no intention of selling, don't need the money, but for Jerry, I'd consider it. My wife wants to get rid of the place." I suspect that like other men whose wives carp about being "fishing widows," Howard believes that not many women love the river. I know better, but I let it pass. After all, Howard holds the keys to prospective river property.

Two days later we are standing up the bluff from Nine-Mile Island at Shawondassee, just up from Massey Station. From Howard's backyard, the view of the Mississippi takes my breath even as it fills the sails of my soul. To the north we see the tip of Nine-Mile, the river meandering on either side of the island and then branching out into cuts where I know it leads to Dead Man's and Menominee sloughs. Farther north, the river curves in a swifter current passing through Frentress Lake across the channel, cutting through limestone bluffs, and I swear I can nearly see all the way up to Minnesota's Lake Itasca from this spot. This day herons and (oddly enough for summer) a pair of eagles soar over the bluffs. I fall in love again, but this time with the river.

More modest than the view, the cottage has two typical small bedrooms with whitewashed faux oak paneling. Like similar homes on rivers or lakes, there is an air of dampness in the basement despite the air conditioner braced in one of the back windows. The kitchen is clean and simple—a good thing, because I'd prefer to spend less time cooking and more time watching the river. Our search up to this point has made it clear that this may be the only place for sale in the next ten years at Shawondassee, and this place is considerably larger than I'd imagined. It's been maintained impeccably, too.

The enormous living room looks out on the river through windows that seem too small for the panorama beyond them. But then, what glass panes could ever hope to hold the Mississippi? Howard makes certain we know this could never be a winter residence, informing us, "No heat." But as a summer cottage, the place is royal.

Howard and his wife have kept it tidy, and it is right over the best vista of this stretch of the river. On the other hand, although I haven't gone public to the family with my deepest desire, I do plot to eventually settle in at the river year-round, and this is definitely not the place to do it. The hilly road up may be impassable in winter snow, and a neighbor tells us that it sometimes washes out in spring flood. With Andrew, Elizabeth, and James still living at home and with Bekah and Jason returning with spouses and their future children, two small bedrooms would be tight, and our finances would be too hard-pressed to add on.

All the same, by the time we head out to the front porch, I resign myself to signing on for the view, acknowledging the shortcomings of the cottage as a permanent residence. Walking out to the porch, Howard points downstream toward Frentress and tells us, "We used to have a place over there at Frentress. Basement flooded every year. I got tired of mucking up, so we ended up here on the bluff."

Like a fetching smile on an otherwise sturdy face, the screen porch creates a handsomeness that I can't resist. The knotty pine deck and walls run the width of the cottage. As we sit on the porch with Howard, sipping lemonade under a pleasantly slow-spinning ceiling fan, I imagine how I could set it up. A chair here facing the river, I think, oak desk in front of it, paper on the right, laptop in front of me on the desk, pen behind my ear (old habits die hard), and the Countess singing "Porgi Amour" from the stereo as I wade knee-deep writing the Great American Nonfiction book. Hey, it could work.

Compared to real estate in town, Howard's asking price seems fair, but it's too high for a second home for us. We have been warned by river folks that when it comes to buying river property, the right price is the one you need to match in order to get the place. "Whatever it's worth to you, that's what you pay," Joe advises us back at

Graham's Style Store for Men, picking a piece of lint from Jer's collar as he tries on a dress shirt and jacket. Besides, all the charming country antique furniture comes with the Higley deal. Most of all there's beach access. It's down steep rickety steps and on the main channel where no dock will hold, but it is beach access all the same. On top of all this, we know Howard to be a fair businessman, and we trust his price. We tell Howard we'll think about it.

When it rains, it floods. A week later after Jazzercise class, I stop in at the Koffee Kup on Bluff Street just a few blocks from Dubuque's downtown harbor. The shop's real name is Mississippi Mug Bean and Brew House, but those of us who are regulars often refer to it as the Kup, except for Ken. Ken is a potter, so it's natural for him to reshape clay, ideas, and even words. With penetrating dark eyes, unruly dark hair, and his potter pants splattered with this morning's work, he asserts, "I think it's more like a bus stop. People stop in here, pull up a seat for a while, and then head on to other destinations."

I see Judy, her left eyebrow cocked, glance over from her corner table by the window. Her usual uniform of jeans and T-shirt finds her sporting "Support the Arts" across her back. She brushes aside a silver lock of hair from her forehead and seems about to jump into the name game conversation but instead calls out, "Meter maid!" Ken grabs coins off the bar and runs through the front door out to the curb. Judy watches from the window and soon reports, "He got to the meter before she did." Ken returns to the bar amid the cheers of the regulars. Those of us who frequent downtown are vigilant in watching the meters for one another. I once got a ticket and sent it to the city manager's office along with a bill. I figured that the city owed me $78.23 for all the unused time I'd left on meters over the years. I suggested they install a device so that one could get change for her unused time, but for some reason they never responded to my bill.

Returning to the topic of the day, Judy suggests that train station is a more apt nickname for the place, "People come in here and get derailed all the time." Finally, Merrill chimes in, "I think you people have entirely too much time on your hands and too few thoughts in your heads."

As usual, Merrill Toups is behind the bar whistling as he compacts ground espresso into the basket. Today he wears the olive green "Jam the Dam" hat, a souvenir from the outdoor jazz fest that rocks the dam in Bellevue each summer.

As the best coffee meister in town, Merrill is also an artist. He takes all the colors of his patrons—two purple lawyers, a bright blue substitute teacher, a silver metal artist, the red potter, a couple of mauve businesswomen, and a green writer/college professor—and paints them into one canvas of conversation. No one is a stranger for long at the Kup, as Merrill pours out his calming laid-back attitude, offsetting the caffeine.

Merrill is a river man with Louisiana roots. He learned to make gumbo from his mom near Lafayette in Cajun Country and stays connected to his crawfish and shrimp suppliers somewhere near the Bayou—only he knows precisely where. Yearly, when the Chili Cook-Off draws thousands to this Bluff Street region in hopes of finding the Best Chili Ever, Kup regulars know that Merrill's gumbo pot is simmering at the back of the coffee shop.

 Merril's Pretty Good Cajun Gumbo

Handed down to him by his mother, Audrey Lendry Toups, of Youngsville, Louisiana.

Ingredients
1 medium chicken
1 lb. andouille sausage, sliced (or smoked sausage)
1 cup cooking oil
1 cup flour
1 large onion, chopped ⎫ *In Cajun country, onion, celery,*
4 stalks celery, chopped ⎬ *and bell pepper together are*
1 bell pepper ⎭ *known as the "trinity."*
½ cup fresh parsley, chopped
1 package (16 oz.) frozen chopped okra, cooked
1 tsp. thyme
1 tsp. red cayenne pepper
1 bay leaf
Gumbo file (ground sassafras) for garnish

Boil chicken in about 2 gallons of water until meat starts to come off the bone. Remove chicken from pot, debone, and save the stock. Heat oil in a large Dutch oven or a stockpot with a thick bottom. Whisk in the flour and stir constantly with whisk or a roux spoon (spoon with flat edge). When roux becomes the color of an old copper penny, add the trinity. Be careful, as the vegetables will produce much steam when they hit the hot roux. Lower heat and simmer for about 10 minutes. Add parsley, garlic, thyme, cayenne pepper, and bay leaf. Stir and simmer for 10 minutes. Stir in chicken stock. Bring to a slow boil. Reduce heat and simmer for 30 minutes. Add chicken, sausage, and cooked okra. Stir and simmer for 30 minutes. Taste. Add Tabasco or Creole seasoning, if desired. Serve over rice. Sprinkle gumbo file on top. *C'est bon, cher!*

On a normal day with the place so full of patrons, I would continue to exchange friendly jibes with him and the others, search out the latest town gossip gleaned from the *Dubuque Telegraph Herald,* check out new art on the walls, and chat about which band is playing over at Isabella's, an uptown bar located in the historic Ryan House. But today I'm getting down to business. At breakfast this morning, Jerry suggested that perhaps we should give up the hunt for riverfront property, that maybe it just wasn't the right time after all. Second-guessing always makes me nervous.

"What'll it be today, Kate?" Merrill interrupts my worrying. I spy Fran at the far end of the bar. Before I even place my order for "the usual," I pop out with it: "Franny! You ever hear of places on the river for sale?" Fran Henkels, a lawyer who favors fine wine and gourmet cuisine over Bud and fried catfish, used to spend weekends boating the river, but I haven't seen him out on it in ages. I don't know what came over me in asking him. I suppose I was just that desperate.

"Stone cottage at Frentress. Foreclosure," he whispers, as if the regulars and the other two patrons in the shop—an older woman wearing a flower print dress sipping an iced latte and her grandson downing Mountain Dew—might pounce on the deal if they heard. And he's right. They might. Even Merrill, convivial Merrill who is quite satisfied with his house in Bellevue, looks like a contender to me just now. I know that at any moment, he will lace up the gloves and come out from his corner of the ring. I am sure I see him leaning forward across the coffee bar to get a closer listen. That's how coveted Frentress properties are.

The cut to Frentress Lake.

Frentress Lake is actually a slough of the Mississippi. Around these parts, "lake" refers to backwaters that don't empty back out into the river, that have only a single "cut," or lane of water, connecting them to the main channel. The water in such places is slower with less current, safer. Commercial fishermen joke that Frentress is one of the best "bass holes" on the upper river.

Fran tells me that the bank will likely be forced into taking back the cottage from its owner. I motion him to follow me to a less-populated corner of the Kup. Glaring at the regulars, Merrill, grandma, and the kid, I ask him to fill me in further. According to Fran, the property should be coming up for bid at the end of the month. "You didn't hear it from me," he warns as he grabs his cinnamon mocha from the counter and leaves. Before exiting, he pauses with his hand on the knob, "Call Tom Reilly, vice president at East Dubuque Savings Bank. They're handling it."

I phone Jerry at the office, at home, on his cell. He's having one of *those* days, I groan to myself. He will be out of contact for hours, off on the site where he checks in on the construction of the new museum and aquarium he directs. He's been putting in sixty- to seventy-hour weeks for two years now, so I'm glad we've arranged a date uptown later that night at Swingfest, the annual celebration hosted by Duke's Place jazz club. When I tell him about Fran and Frentress, he's on the cell phone within seconds calling the president of the foreclosing bank at home. "These are desperate times, Kate," he grins apologetically as he dials the man at home on a Friday night. But President Bonnet is out of town on family vacation on the river. Next we phone Tom Reilly.

Not publicly advertised, it will be sealed bids of those who hear through word of mouth, he tells us. "You won't even know what the bids are in order to beat them," Tom explains, tapping his pencil in the background. What's worse, we have to wait until the foreclosure goes through. Six more weeks. "First property at Frentress next to the creek, the limestone one," he directs us.

Even before the Blue Band strikes up at Swingfest, we are in our car heading to Illinois. We have to make sure. Driving into the lake region, we take the curve to the left. Leaving the blacktop and continuing on gravel, Jerry and I keep our eyes straight ahead. We don't dare look at one another for fear of jinxing it.

The only stone house we know of at Frentress is *the* stone house, the one we discovered ten years earlier while boating the lake, the one we have always claimed was "our" dream cottage, the best place on the river for us, our nirvana. "It's probably some old dilapidated former outhouse," I say to Jerry as he nods in agreement, neither of us risking to hope that it could possibly be *the* house.

Pulling into the sandy grass at the back of "our" limestone house, the one we have only boated past for ten years and merely dreamed of until this evening, Jer is the first to speak, "It looks empty." Normally loath to trespass, we are each out of the car and up the lawn before the car doors slam. Taped to the back door, we find notices from the power company threatening to cut off electricity—a good sign. We round the yard to the front of the cottage, the side facing the lake. With my hands bridging between my temples and the plate glass patio doors, I squint to see through the reflections, hoping there are no signs of life inside, "Not a stick of furniture. It's empty." Nearly convinced that this house is indeed the one coming up for bid, Jerry is already on the beach reporting, "The retaining wall took a real hit in the spring flood."

Having grown up on Lake Michigan where ten low years are followed by ten high, where your backyard erodes eighth-inch by eighth-inch rather than yard by yard as it does on the swifter, more powerful Mississippi, I feel zero at the bone at his words. We'd just been through one of the worst floods of the century on the upper river. Although we'd helped friends downriver sandbag and clean up afterward, all I'd known of the flood at Frentress was a little water in Rita and Dave's basement. They live on the river there and wisely have their furnace and water heater raised above flood levels. It didn't seem so bad.

But here, two trees lean over the bank on one side of the yard at a forty-five-degree angle to the water, their roots fully exposed. On the other side, another tree's branches sweep right down into the river's surface. The railroad ties that were constructed to hold the ten-foot bank are askew and ripped down to bare soil every few feet. Hoping to hold back the bank, someone had dumped a load of rocks into a pile at one point, but since they didn't form a wall, they'd fallen down into the shore, the better to harpoon boats landing on the beach or to rip into the feet of hapless swimmers.

Nonetheless I can feel it rising, that irresistible urge to do something foolish, to bet the farm and buy the place. I know Jerry is feeling the same thing. Besides, we rationalize, if Joe, whose intelligence and wit we respect, has persisted in living on this slough his whole life, it can't be as dotty an idea as it seems (even if you don't own the land under your own house). "If Joe can do it, so can we," becomes our mantra during the next few weeks.

"That's the one." With these words, Bonnet confirms the limestone house on the phone the next week when I call to check in with him, now that he's finally off that houseboat of his. (Really, how *could* he have gone on vacation at a time like this?) Bonnet is both the banker handling the foreclosure as well as the family manager for the Frentress properties. True to his word to keep the bidding fair, he won't play his hand on what the property might be worth or what to bid, no matter how many different ways I try to wheedle a hint out of him.

I solicit information and advice, visiting neighbors up and down the lake, but discreetly so. Because I don't want to leak the news that the house may come up for bid, I ask about the recent history of homes on the lake. They know I'm a writer, so they presume I'm doing an article for the local newspaper.

Worried that we'd be taking advantage of some poor widow down on her knees at the mercy of the corporate Snidely Whiplash banking world, I'm pleased to find that Frentress folks are quick to correct that image. Although their opinions of the former owner and builder of the house vary widely, they all confirm one thing: He's in prison. Some say that regardless of his legal problems, he was a loyal friend, "Dusty was the first to help out if you were ever in trouble." Dusty's son, who has been managing the house since his father went to jail, wishes us well in our bid. He admits on the phone that the place has "bad karma" for him.

"I'll go see Bonnet," Joe promises. Bonnet's own house at Frentress shares the back lane with ours—or what we hope will be ours. If we keep our noses clean and make it clear that the beagle and three teenagers won't be too rowdy, maybe we'll have a chance. Joe makes no promise of persuading Bonnet, but it can't hurt, we reason. I fantasize that Tom Reilly is wrong or that there's still a chance that Bonnet will sell the place outright, swayed by what a nice respectable couple we are. "It's open to anyone who wants to bid, but we're not advertising," Bonnet sets me straight on the phone.

Not having met the man, I picture Bonnet as one of those cinematic overseers of sharecroppers who cackles in extorting exorbitant sums while giving the poor disenfranchised dolts virtually worthless plots of land. I have only heard him referred to by his last name, surely a bad sign. Is he so high and mighty that he gazes down on the peon renters? As we pull into the sandy gravel lane at the back of the house, he approaches our van. Seeing him dressed in the uniform of bankers—dark pants, a stark, crisp white shirt, and a conservative tie—I am sure my image of him is correct (albeit stereotypical).

With prematurely graying hair and a smile that rivals Tom Sawyer's boyishness, he greets us, "I'm Steve." He has a first name, I laugh to myself. Steve may be a darn good bank president, I reflect, but there is nothing in his kindly demeanor that suggests CEO-ness or the rush-rush of the business world. He has been through this before, I realize, the touring of people who would give their youngest child in trade for a residence on the river, and he is sympathetic.

When he shows us through the inside of the house, I delight at the sight of four glass double patio doors giving the front of the house an enormously vast view of the river. The sun showering in through those doors shimmers the great room with an airiness so luminous that I grow light-headed. Whatever the truth of the Dusty stories, I know this much: Stone by stone, with his own hands, Dusty designed and built a breathtaking place that reveals a man who couldn't get enough of the Mississippi, who had to surround himself with river views on three sides and with native limestone throughout interior walls, the chimney, and the exterior face. People are complicated beings with virtues and vices often at odds within the same heartbeat. Whatever his civil and societal crimes may have been, I decide, Dusty must have a river soul.

Lowering my eyes from the patio doors, I gasp again, this time at the sight of mold circling the walls at the one-foot level around the entire first floor. Everything below that mark—drywall, woodwork, floors—is murky, spongy, obviously needing to be replaced. I can't help but recall the briny lariat inside the Saltair mosque beach pavilion left by the Great Salt Lake flooding some years earlier. From its very roots, I feel the hair on my head begin to stand up.

Steve tells us that unlike many of the houses at Frentress, this one is low enough it flooded for the first time last spring. Even in low flood years—which is every year—water flows right through the basement. "The wise owner opens those extra wide basement doors and lets the Mississippi in," he explains. To pump, to try and keep the river out and the basement dry, is to invite disaster, since pressure outside the foundation will collapse the basement walls.

Empty Budweiser bottles are scattered throughout the house, pink gum sticks to the carpet, and there are obvious trails of a cat stalking a herd of mice. Although this place was once "the showcase of Frentress Lake," no one has lived here for over a year, Steve explains. I can't help but think of Howard's: clean-and-tidy Howard's, without-signs-of-river-flood-or-rodent-life Howard's. And Howard's words, about emigrating up the hill to escape water at his Frentress cottage, echo in my mind like the steps of an avenger in heavy pursuit.

The next week, Jerry and I return to Howard's cottage for another look. Compared to Frentress, Howard's place boasts the more majestic view, the writer's front porch, and closer proximity to Carol's burgers. We could be happy here. Best of all, we could move right in without renovating. But it would be for summers only, and toting our prospective grandchildren down those long rickety steps is forbidding. Thinking of our teenage drivers daily making the trip from Howard's to jobs in town along an often foggy, winding highway, too, quickens my pulse. But this is a bird in the hand, however, and as long as we meet Howard's price, the place is ours without the emotional hassle of closed bidding—to say nothing of having to clean up and remodel from last year's flood.

Joined by Joe and his wife, Ruth, later that week, we boat over to Frentress, tie up to the railroad ties sticking out from the front bank, scale the jagged concrete steps, leap the two-foot gap between the top step and backyard, and again peek in the windows. The house with two modest bedrooms and potential for another two, huge first-floor front rooms, and a grand bedroom suite in which you could open your eyes in the morning and see the Mississippi beyond your feet, is year-round-able without doubt. It has heat.

Of course, the view at Frentress of a back slough lake running two miles long by half a mile across isn't nearly as awe-inspiring as the view at Howard's, where you can see a full fifteen-barge tow heading upstream.

Then again, thinking of the strong currents of the main channel at Howard's, I recall that even golden retrievers wear life jackets on that part of the river, whereas at Frentress the water is much calmer, safer.

Too, at Frentress there is the little matter of replacing drywall, doors, floors, water heaters, and raising the wiring up out of the basement, but that is doable, we agree.

That the basement floods every time the river is above fifteen feet (which is every spring) is distressing.

I begin to feel like a ping-pong ball the longer Joe, Ruth, Jerry, and I paddle back and forth between the two choices.

When you've got two fishing poles in the water and they both spring at the same time, deciding which to reel in and which to let go is daunting. You might have just an old shoe on the end of one of the lines. From the surface, it's impossible to tell which line is bass and which is boot. What finally tips the scale in our decision, however, is our mutual obsession. Jerry and I each claim various places at the Frentress house—the loft on the third floor, the first-floor apex of four patio doors, the back den with its double-window view of the side creek, the upstairs grand suite—all as desk locations for our writing.

As if this weren't enough, Ruth reminds us that at the Frentress July Fourth celebration, "There are no spectators because everyone is in our parade." Pass up a chance to dress as Lady Liberty and carry a torch? No way. The karma—for us—is good.

Knowing there may be as many as one hundred bidders or as few as five, Jerry and I struggle over what figure to put down on that white sheet of legal paper for the bank. When I tell him that sheet of paper could become either our river residence birth certificate or our death warrant, he lifts an eyebrow and suggests that perhaps I'm being a bit extreme. In a saner moment, I'd have agreed with him, but not just now.

Watching him slather his toast with raspberry jam one morning shortly before the bids are due, I scribble a figure on the back of my napkin and slide it over to him asking, "How about this?" I've written a dollar amount echoing the figure he'd suggested shortly before falling asleep the night before. Together we monkey with the dimes and pennies until it includes the numerals of our birth dates and wedding date. Although he is not any more superstitious than I am, without any comparable property to judge by, we both figure it's a coin toss and we may as well go with it.

We are not materialistic people, given our American culture as a whole. I drive an eight-year-old Mercury, and Jerry still wears a pair of green socks he owned in college nearly three decades ago. Our furniture is the castoff of our parents from twenty-five years ago, and we've lived in the same house for nearly as long. I'm not sure I could legitimately call us frugal, but material things don't seem to matter so much to us. Consequently, the figure seems nervously high to me. Counting a small inheritance and money put away bit by bit since our wedding day, we're like kids spilling out socks full of change onto the table. If we bite the bullet on other spending, we could do this.

Given what we have heard from neighbors about the sales of other cottages at Frentress, I can't help but imagine the crowd at the bank at the bid opening. I see a lady in the front row catching her straw sun hat as it topples from her head, shaken by her convulsing guffaws as Steve Bonnet reads our bid. Bonnet's own voice goes hoarse from astonishment as he reads the figure. He, too, breaks into laughter and mutters something like, "I'll be damned. What city people won't pay!" I imagine our bid is more than $20,000 over the next closest.

But then Joe's words about paying what it's *worth to us* run through my head like a radio jingle I can't stop from repeating. Maybe the figure isn't high enough, high enough, high enough? Now I envision that lady in the straw hat in the front row rolling her eyes and pronouncing "Cheapskates!" as she edges her chair as far away from Jerry and me as possible. Bonnet throws down our envelope and grinds it under his wingtip, so insulted is he at the low bid.

Or worse, maybe we'll miss the mark by ten or twenty dollars. For the first time, I begin to fully understand the term *wild card*. We decide to sleep on it.

The night before the bids will be unsealed and read in public, I wake up out of a deep sleep, elbow Jerry until he opens one eye, and tell him, "I think that on the bid sheet I might have put those numbers down in reverse order and moved the decimal point two places to the left," I confess. Patting me on the hip, muttering something like, "'It's only a dream, Kate,'" he returns to his own restlessness, uttering phrases in his sleep. "High water" and "Get the bucket," I think I hear him say.

Comforted that he, too, is having nightmares about the bid, I fall back asleep to images of sipping Pinot Grigio on the patio with friends on a warm summer evening as we nibble dill Brie on crackers and listen to Mozart. I see the string quartet set up on the grass just below the patio. As they play, the black quarter notes from their violins and cello rise up over their heads and float into the ears of those of us sitting on the patio chatting. They continue until a low-flying bat comes squealing into our midst, entangling itself in my hair. It screeches into my ear.

I turn off the alarm clock. It's time to get dressed and head to campus to face my morning college literature class. After the tremors of last night, I look forward to class. Stephanie will have wonderful insights about the assigned reading. Tom will challenge the status quo ideas, bless him. No matter that two students will confuse fiction with nonfiction (terms my own children accuse me of blurring as a writer), or that Sally in the back row will not have read today's assignment, a wonderful short story by Flannery O'Connor, one of the best writers from the Mississippi River. At least their eagerness to learn and creatively interpret literature will refocus me from that which has been uppermost in my mind for weeks. Bids will be opened at the bank this morning. Since I have class, Jerry will be present at the opening without me. I'll carry the cell, but he's not to call until 9:16 when class is over.

The students are eager to sidetrack me this morning. Knowing they will learn better if they think they've detoured me from today's lesson plan for a while, I indulge them for five minutes. Besides, it's only the second week of school, and we are all still suffering the loss of summer.

"Why would you buy a house when you don't even own the land under it?" Colleen is the first to question my sanity. Scott points out our folly further, "And a place that floods!" I have to admit that it doesn't make much sense to me, either. But then, I suppose, there's a lack of reason behind many of the things and people we love most. In fact, perhaps we love things like a river *because* of the wart on its face, *because* it floods, and *because* we cannot contain it.

I tell students the story of Poster Honey, more to satisfy my own self-interrogation rather than theirs. When I was in college in the seventies, nearly all the boys had the same poster on their dorm room walls. I dubbed her "Poster Honey." With perfectly straight blond hair, eyes so blue-green you wanted to swim in them, a velvet complexion, a perfectly turned-up nose, and a smile captivating and potent, she was dazzling. She was the ultimate vision about which most middle-class white heterosexual men fantasized.

But Poster Honey was the composite of 126 different women whose "best features" a photographer had touched up and airbrushed into this one persona. In real life, I explain further to the students, among those 126 women were dimples, scars, curved smiles, thin lips, protruding chins, upturned eyebrows, freckles, raucous laughter, and more. Those features, the ones that didn't get airbrushed into the poster, I claim, were the ones that made people individuals. Those features, I preach at them, were the ones that made it worthwhile to actually know those women. "Perfection is boring," I am on a roll now. Students wince as I quote an older friend of mine, "Never trust anyone without wrinkles."

"Just so," I continue (eyeing Colleen, who is about to drift off, and Jeff, ready to poke her with his pencil), "the Mississippi is at its best when it's at its worst—in flood." I almost start to believe my own preaching by this point. "Now, let's talk about the protagonist

Shore Acres house constructed to withstand flood on first floor.

in 'A Good Man Is Hard to Find,'" I suggest. After my waxing on and on, the students are relieved to turn to their literature texts. It's a good class, and I am surprised to check the clock and find we have only minutes left.

At 9:16 a.m. sharp, the cell phone rings. "Hello, Katie, my dear?" Jer begins more sweetly than honey. I am silent. He doesn't continue. Is he preparing me for sad news? "Tell me!" I shout into the phone. "There were seven bids altogether," he says. I am silent. "The top bids were within a couple thousand of each other," he baits me further. I am silent again. Realizing I am in no mood for the game, he finally reports, "We landed a great big smelly catfish with huge whiskers, Kate, right on the deck. We won the bid!"

Crossing Over

Having purchased paradise on the other side of the bridge from Iowa at Frentress Lake, Illinois, I discover the hell that Eden brings. Since it's too cold for a boat now in this late midwestern fall, I travel across the river by road these days, just in time for repair work to begin on the Julien Dubuque Bridge. Department of Transportation workers are removing a chunk of the south lane and diverting traffic to a single lane, this lane-switching syncopated by a construction worker rotating her STOP/SLOW warning sign.

In my more reflective moments, I think of this sign as the physical reminder of how, perhaps, I should have been more cautious about getting a place on the floodplain. Then, too, I know that had I been more cautious, I'd have been doomed to live up the hill forever, safe but not sound. After all, what is life without risk?

In the main part of my days, however, those filled with the practicalities and constantly racing the clock, I know that the STOP/SLOW sign is just a sign that regulates vehicular traffic and not a metaphor for anything at all. Regardless of the sign's deeper meanings, I spend a lot of drive time these days waiting on the bridge to go east. I'm coming to sympathize with my fellow "Easties" who have been putting up with bridge work for decades. With no other route across the river for miles, patience is not merely a virtue; it's a necessity.

Working on the house at Frentress, I make four to six round trips daily between the uplands life in Iowa and the river floodplain in Illinois. Some days I rack up close to three hours sitting on the bridge in my trusty Mercury Mystique. With the thrill of being suspended hundreds of feet over the third largest river in the world fizzling by the fourth trip of the morning, I find myself daydreaming about television. Yes, television.

Not normally much of a viewer, last night I became mesmerized by the blue tube as I brushed with my battery-driven toothbrush. First there was a fanfare of harps and trumpets. The smooth-faced host leapt into the incandescent light on stage forming a halo around his body. He closed his eyes meaningfully and leaned his head back precisely fourteen degrees. His chin and mouth grew solemn yet without growing mean. "I'm hearing someone—Bob or Bill or Bim or Betty or Barbara or Bowser?" His left brow wrinkled just a bit, "Something that begins with *B*? Does that have meaning to anyone here?"

I turned off my toothbrush mid-bicuspid when a thin, drawn man of sixty-something in the audience jumped out of his seat hollering, "My sister, her name was Carol." The host-angel, whose eyes have popped wide open like shades snapping up the window, smiled knowingly, took the man's hand, and said, "Yes, I thought so. *C* is the letter next to *B*, and Carol is here next to you right now. She says she's sorry she died. She says she crossed over easily and you shouldn't worry any more about her pain." I started up the toothbrush again and snapped off the TV, but not before the man who talks to dead people made a lasting impression on me.

Now, as I sit on the bridge, again waiting to cross over, I can't help but think of that program. Life is short and before long, like Carol, we all end up on the other side (or at least a host-angel will *say* he's talking to us from beyond the grave). Even waiting on a bridge gives me moments too precious to waste with idle thoughts of last night's television show or on wishing the truck ahead of me had a better exhaust system. How can I use the time? I devise a list of things to do while waiting to cross over:

1. Sort through the glove compartment. This is where anyone would start, still hoping the wait will be short enough that there will be little time for anything more than this to do.

2. Clean out the sticky penny cup and replenish with coins for making donations to city parking meters.

3. Unlock car doors (you never know when the electrical system will fail).

4. Make out two grocery lists—one for home and one for the car, stocking up for future trips over the bridge.

5. Play radio roulette with the kids, betting they won't be able to listen to one entire Chet Atkins tune straight through.

6. Delete office voicemail via cell phone.

7. Give thumbs-up to construction workers, making a mental note to give them as wide a berth as one allows tows and barges on the river below.

8. Test car window push-buttons (see number 3 above).

9. Start a support group with fellow "Easties" caught on the bridge by holding up "conversation" signs to one another in your car windows.

10. Floss.

11. Tell your kids to quit jumping around in the backseat. When you realize there's no one else in the car but you, and it's not your motor quaking the car as if the New Madrid fault is slipping, test door locks and power windows again (see #3 above).

12. Envision having a party. The guests will be DOT and city planners from the Iowa side. The party will be at your house on the Illinois side. Friday at 5:15 pm should do it.

13. Take advantage of the situation and tell your kids "Why did the chicken cross the bridge" jokes. Toss in a few lectures beginning with "When I was your age." Encourage them to join you singing very loudly with Janis on the radio, "Me and Bobby McGee."

14. Write Post-its to yourself to fill the gas tank before taking the trip back.

15. Learn to identify insects by the shape of their splatter on the windshield.

16. Tape-record that novel you've been meaning to write. Make it a three-book series. You've got the time.

17. Knit (multitasking circular needles and a circular steering wheel works astonishingly well).

18. Catch up on the toning exercises (squeeze, squeeze!) you were too late to do at Jazzercise yesterday because you were delayed on the bridge.

19. Release a carrier pigeon with a note to Graham's Style Store for Men begging them to extend their latest sale on boxer shorts long enough for you to get across the bridge.

20. Listen to books on tape, maybe the Old and New Testaments as well as the Koran and the Bhagavad Gita.

21. Call the Body and Soul Spa and make an appointment for a massage—after sitting in one position this long, you'll need it.

22. Watch the Iowa Powerball billboard rise from $27 million to $28 million as it competes with the Illinois Lottery billboard, escalating from $32 million to $34 million.

23. Call in a pledge to National Public Radio just to be able to talk with another human being.

24. Check out the orange life vest buckles and straps (formerly kept in the boat but now stowed on the backseat—just in case).

25. Finally, reconsider the move across the bridge.

Do I *really* want a river residence this badly? I'm willing to slog through floodwaters, hawk over the children to wear life jackets at the beach, renovate the house, and deal with constant interrogations from friends about how in heck we could move onto the floodplain, but this? This waiting?

Then again maybe waiting on a bridge is only a precursor for what comes next. In life, after all, experience doesn't cross over so neatly as it does in fictional stories with their nice tidy plots where obstacles and conflict are overcome, resulting in resolution and conclusion. At least that's what I teach in literature class as students and I chart story lines.

In our real lives, complications rarely end, although they do shift and shimmy and turn inside out like flags flapping from boat docks. Our solutions only rarely solve things "once and for all." Today's divorce lingers with alimony, parental custody, and shared memories. Even moving from one home to another carries over objects that symbolize the life accumulated during tenure in the first house—memories, and the dreams that came true as well as those that did not. These crossings-over require more waiting, more patience than crossing any bridge.

Similarly, maybe we don't get to cross over after death so quickly as traditional religious upbringing might have us believe. Perhaps I'll be stuck sitting out the next phase in afterlife in a compact Ford on some cosmic bridge with the gulfs of human life streaming beneath me. Come to think of it, that bridge may be what Sister John

Mary in grade school meant by "purgatory." If I do have to sit on that bridge, at least I'll have had plenty of purgatory practice. And if I do wait, I'm hoping that what lies on the other side is as heavenly as living on the Mississippi River.

A River Runs through It

"I'll take it off your hands anytime," Jummy Hail offers on the phone one week after we win the bid on our river dream house. Jummy sends us photos of our charming stone cottage. In his photos, however, there are no gravel roads, no steps leading up to the back door, no basement windows, and no lawn whatsoever. A big dead fish floats in the water that tops the back doorsteps. Although we'd already been told the house took on water in the flood of 2001, seeing concrete proof in these images is upsetting.

Surely there was grass somewhere in the photographs of our property taken only months earlier, I think as I gaze at the photos in Jerry's extended fingers, but in the pictures all I see is water, water everywhere. Completely surrounded by the Mississippi, the cottage appears as an island complete with its very own dinghy tied up to the back doorknob. Although Jerry and I are shell-shocked speechless as we stare at the photographs, with ESP surety I know we are wondering the exact same thing: "What have we gotten ourselves into?"

I remind myself that Jummy was the next highest bidder. He'd finagled for months to get his hands on the house at Frentress Lake and was terribly disappointed when we won the bid. I recall, too, that when the river reached twenty feet last spring, the former resident had walked off the property without sandbagging. I also tell myself that the river hadn't been that high for thirty-six years (since '65). Even in '93, the next highest flood year on our stretch of river, the house stayed dry.

All the same, as we pass the flood photos back and forth between us, Jerry and I give serious thought to taking Jummy's offer. Despite all my bravado during the bid process and patting myself on the back as a "true river rat," the undeniable proof of these snapshots gets to me. Recalling the muddy residue forming a noose of mold one foot from the floor around the circumference of the entire first floor, I grumble to myself, "Let Hail deal with it."

"Remember the weekend I was going to ask your dad for your hand in marriage?" Jerry reminds me (okay, it was the early seventies, and we weren't *that* liberated yet). That Easter weekend, Lake Michigan ascended to the height of its ten-year rise. Combined with saturation from unusually heavy rainfalls, the basement at our lake house north of Milwaukee flooded. For weeks prior to our leaving college life behind to travel home to my parents' house for the weekend, Jerry and I drafted what he'd say to my dad. For the entire four hours driving home from college, we rehearsed pretend scripts with one another. "Don't forget to tell him the part about how you love me more than the sun, moon, and stars," I coached.

Instead of sitting on the edge of the leather Barcalounger in my father's den and impressing him with plans of providing for his daughter, however, Jerry spent the weekend in the basement hip-wading through water. He primed the pump as my mother directed our flood-control efforts (okay, it was the early seventies, and she was *that* liberated). With every bucket of water he bailed, he also bailed out another practice speech. Now he had the added advantage of mom's advice. "Make sure you tell him that part about having a job with a future," she tutored.

Although Jerry won't admit it, I've always believed that as a young man of twenty-two he found it more preferable to face Lake Michigan's fury lapping against the basement steps than to face my father. By the time Sunday rolled around, both the floodwaters and my father's resistance were on the decline.

"Our roots are in floods." Jerry selects his words carefully, attempting to bolster his own courage as well as mine. I have to admit to myself that we have a history of water flowing through our lives—and our basements.

We'd been warned about buying our historic 1854 Federalist house in town twenty-two years ago, too. There was no clear title, a three-foot section of the house rested on the neighbor's property, and even the seller's real estate agent admitted that the basement "Gets seepage now and again." But with its marble fireplaces, spacious dining room, and sprawling yard full of fir trees and weeping willows, this old house reminded us of those we'd each grown up in.

Despite the lawyer's advice—and our own common sense—we bought the place, banking on the dream. So we'd had our share of plunking down more money to buy the strip of land underneath the house, of plastering and painting every square inch in the place, of replacing the furnace, the roof, and all the carpeting—to say nothing of sopping up after spring rains and building up the ground around the perimeter to prevent further seepage. Nonetheless, twenty-two years later, we agreed, we'd been wise to be foolish.

That house wasn't even near the river.

Figuring I've been a fool for lesser things, I screw my courage to the sticking place and resolve to dive in headfirst. Besides, this time our lawyer tells us, "As your lawyer, I advise you to run away from this Frentress rental deal. As a Dubuquer, I'll tell you that if you don't take the property, I will." Structural engineers advise rip-rap to halt front bank erosion, a local naturalist says let the river rip through, and our Frentress neighbor, Kermit, tells us salvation resides in railroad ties for the waterfront. I name the cottage "A River Runs through It," indicating my wish to work with the river instead of against it.

Jerry and I tell Jummy to go jump in the river.

Determined to stay, to find a rhythm natural to both the river and us, we begin the cleanup from last spring's high water. I had been a mere guest at last spring's flood, helping friends swab out their homes and dry out their marina diners. As uplanders, our son Andrew and I crossed the bridge regularly after school for nearly six weeks to help Arnie and Sandy squeegee the Mississippi out of the Dive In, hand out sandwiches as part of the Red Cross relief efforts, and empathize with folks at Shore Acres who were hoisting water heaters and pianos up on pulleys to keep them out of harm's way.

At the end of each day, however, Andrew and I headed back across the bridge and up the hill to our cozy, dry house high above the floodplain. Now, only months later, with the river nineteen feet lower than it had been in May, we are in our newly acquired river house shoveling out mud, bleaching out mold, replacing floors and drywall, and washing away the silt from a house that had been abandoned before the crest at twenty-six feet, five inches.

Floodplain house where the river may run through it.

Spotting Jerry ready to fire up the power washer and me carrying debris from the basement, Dee Bierie pads across the beach offering the Frentress version of Welcome Wagon gifts: yellow vinyl gloves. "You really shouldn't touch the muck with your bare hands." She knows. Dee and her husband have been cleaning up after spring floods for years at their house across the creek that runs between our properties.

Joe, our friend who runs the clothing store in Dubuque and lives a few houses up at Frentress, drives in that same afternoon astride his trusty tractor, offering to haul the old drenched sofa from the basement. It's full of rat's nests, I just know it. Decked out in a snappy new blue dress shirt, wool suit pants, and leather loafers, Joe is the height of fashion even when he's doing hard labor. He teaches Jerry and me how to prime the water pump and get it working even though there's a hole in the tank big enough for an elephant to wiggle through. Actually, it's only large enough for a worm, but elephant or worm, any size hole means the pump loses pressure, making it worthless.

In the early weeks after winning the bid, though, it is mainly just Jerry and me, side by side, scraping, scrubbing, hauling, and pausing occasionally to grunt, groan, or screw up our noses in disgust. Happily the last owner had pulled up the carpets, but even laying those out again is anything but pleasant. Mice had taken up residence in the abandoned house and evidence of them is everywhere. Droppings stick tenaciously to the fibers of the rolled-up carpets, the kitchen drawers are decorated with their spoor, and dead bodies float in the toilet.

We roll up our sleeves, accustom our noses to the task of pitching out the dead fish in the basement, and call Josh.

Josh Knepper is one of those industrious young people who works forty-hour weeks on house construction and then puts in another twenty so that he can one day afford his own house. Also a member of the National Guard, Josh isn't always available for outside work, but we are lucky. We find him at a time when neither the Guard nor others knock at his off-duty door, and he agrees to help us make the place livable.

Understand that Jerry and I are the grateful recipients of family giveaways for most of the furniture we own. When his parents died some years ago, we gratefully accepted the Victorian sofa, mahogany pier mirror, and marble-top oak tables. Little did it matter to me that they didn't match the castaways from my own mom and dad's downsizing years earlier: the white faux French bedroom furniture, the maple "Ferbs chair" (so named for my piano teacher, Mr. Ferber, whose perch it was during lessons), and two "colonial" maple armchairs fashioned more in the style of the 1950s than the 1770s.

My lackadaisical attitude toward home decorating was evident, too, when we last bought a house and moved into it. I pronounced the navy blue wallpaper with black and fuchsia flowers hung by the former owners "good 'nuff" and found no need to change curtains or carpets for over a decade. The olive green porcelain sink and stove hood still ensconced in that kitchen are testament enough.

In a rare mania of believing that I'd acquired design techniques, I once boldly took charge of wallpapering the small parlor room in our historic house. I selected two patterns in forest green, cranberry, and white in swirly patterns—one for above the chair railing, and a compatible paper for below. What could go wrong?

Jerry, expert in renovating historic buildings and clamming boats, and creating "walls of water" for fish in his aquarium, balked, "I'm not sure those designs will work together, Kate." I volleyed back, "That's what you know." He may know aquariums, preservation, and museums, but he's no Martha Stewart.

After all, this is a man who'd looked down at his feet during a board meeting to discover he had on one black shoe and one brown. He also reveled in garage sales just in case there was a Green River knife buried in the belly of a plaster of Paris pig. Was he to be trusted?

I held my turf.

Because our nineteenth-century house was plumb-line challenged, we'd hired Mike and Tom to hang wallpaper. On the day of the papering, Mike and Tom awaited my arrival in the room silently. They stared at the floor, keeping their eyes from meeting my own. I walked in and burst out laughing, "Yikes, the circus has come to town." Mike and Tom were relieved. Despite their good craftsmanship, the room was gaudier than a sideshow act.

The only one to blame was me. I resolved two things. First, I would never again trust my opinion on anything bigger than a bedspread. Second, I'd go to Mautz Paints the next day to find a matching shade of paint to obliterate the mess below the chair rail. Given subsequent years of ribbing I've received as the "circus ringleader of the parlor," I don't go gently into the good night of interior decorating.

True Capricornian that I am, there are more fundamentals than frills in my cadre of talents. I don't even like shopping. To be faced with fashionable color palates is beyond me. Suddenly I have to *care* about brass or stainless steel, pulls or knobs, and deciphering the difference between "white pine" and "bleached hickory" wood stains.

Dusty, the former owner and builder of the house, we are told, was not a tall man. The graceful but low arches bisecting the great room on the first floor prove it. At six-foot-four, Jerry is the Mutt to Dusty's Jeff, blamming into those arches at every turn. As we lay tape measures on the floor pacing off our grandiose dreams for renovation, Jerry strides from the fireplace to the opposite wall only to bruise his temples. Another time, the arch assaults his left ear.

Although I'd come to see these arches as the wings of seagulls, Jerry sees them as great plaster wing dams waiting to strike out and knock his keel senseless. We agree that of all the structural changes we might make, the lowest arch must be raised first.

Other "challenges" face us, too (this becomes Jerry's favorite euphemism for "problems," the more we work on the project). At the back of the house is the only room in the entire house without a view of the river—the kitchen. "A real bachelor pad," Rita up the road terms the house, because of the kitchen.

More than two people in the kitchen would be a crowd. Unlike the feeling of airiness apparent in the big front rooms, it feels dark and dank back there. As I stand next to the space for the refrigerator, I feel as though I've been banished. After inviting Jerry to join me in making *every* meal if the kitchen stays as is, renovation is a soft sell. We also need to add a first-floor bathroom. The old kitchen, stashed in the back, seems a perfect place.

The kitchen will move up to the great room alongside the spacious living room. Tossing salad while looking out at the lake is too tempting for even Jerry to resist, and before I know it, we are at a local merchant's buying kitchen cabinets while Josh is off measuring bathroom fixtures. Our plans get bigger by the minute—nearly like the Mississippi itself, rising in spring, out of control.

The house has only two bedrooms. With three children still living at home and two adult children visiting frequently, this simply will not do. The biggest bedroom is nearly the size of a basketball court. In fact, we hear rumors that Dusty's son and his friends used to play basketball up there. Accustomed to the twelve-by-twelve-foot confines of our bedroom at the old house, Jerry and I agree that we could easily carve out another room by installing new walls. The unfinished loft adjacent to the biggest bedroom, too, offers the promise of being finished. Although a traditional staircase up to the loft won't fit in the space available, Josh is a genius in creating a spiral set of steps. Four bedrooms and a first-floor den that can double as a guest room will work, we decide.

These renovations are not nearly as *challenging* as what lay ahead of us, however. We have yet to tell our five children—Rebekah, Jason, James, Elizabeth, and Andrew—that we would move the following spring out of the house where we'd lived for more than twenty years.

"You've always wanted to get back to living on water, Mom," Rebekah understands perfectly upon hearing the news when I phone. Making her own way in a rapidly changing life, she is quick to cheer on our adventure. Living near Chicago with her enthusiastic husband, she is about to have her first baby. This will be our first grandchild, so I wander from the topic easily in order to check up on how pregnancy is treating her. Her head is full of hypno-birthing techniques and the psychological disadvantages of pacifiers. Our phone conversation quickly shifts to discussing her latest doctor's appointment.

Jason phones from Iowa City. A nature boy since his earliest days when he refused to abandon digging for worms in the yard in order to come inside for spaghetti dinner, he is instantly in favor of the idea. "When I come home to visit, we'll canoe up the slough," he rhymes. As a teenager, he relished the idea of one day becoming a forest ranger. Once an insect-gatherer, always an insect-gatherer. He'll travel to Washington, D.C., next year to attend law school, so he's already in the mind-set of moving.

But both of these older children have already moved to apartments of their own in other cities.

As the youngest, at twelve years of age, and perhaps most pliable, Andrew is instantly excited by the idea. A longtime aspiring river rat, the only of our five children to actually grow up on boats and beaches since toddlerhood, he reminds me of myself at his age.

Back in those Lake Michigan days, beginning at age five, I rose each morning and—before pancakes or eggs over easy, before brushing teeth or changing clothes, almost before opening my eyes—I was on the beach saying good morning to the lake. Even through high school and during vacations home from college, my daily routine began with listening to the lake. There was nothing romantic or poetic about it; it was just something I did to feel refreshed, like taking a morning shower.

Just so, from the time he was three, the one obstinacy the normally pleasant Andrew demonstrated was when I tried to get him to come in off the river after a full day on the islands. At three, he'd run and hide back in the marshes at the tip of the island. At five, he'd threaten to get himself adopted by another family, one staying longer on the beach. By six, he'd try to bribe me, "I won't eat any candy for a week if I can stay out here longer... okay, for a month!"

When it came to leaving the river after a day of boating, Andrew dug his toes into the mud. So when we told him of the new home, his only consternation was, "Why do we have to wait until spring to move?" But then he's lived fewer years in the old house than have Elizabeth and James.

Middle child James explains that he really doesn't want to move from the old house. Indeed, he thinks we are a bit crazed to move into a house where the largest American river runs through the basement each spring. But he is not fiercely opposed to it; his practicality and natural bent toward mathematics and numbers are apparent from his response: "I'll move out in two years anyway, once I graduate from college." As agreeable as he tries to be, however, it is clear that he finds the prospect of sharing a bedroom with a brother seven years his junior less than ideal. For the first season at the house, he will be off in Prien studying German, however, so he's focusing more on Eurail passes and charting out where he can find Figaro and Cozi on the European stage than on river concerns.

Hardest hit by the river property acquisition—and the prospect of moving—is Elizabeth. "It'll be my last summer in high school," she moans, "and no one is going to want to drive all the way out to Frentress to hang out." If you're from a big city, you'd find the 6.2 miles between the two houses laughable when termed as "all that way." But if you live in a region like we do, where the other end of town is 3.6 miles away at most, teenagers find spans of more than a couple of miles insurmountable.

They'll cut slack to friends who genuinely live in a whole other town like Peosta or Galena; they'll actually drive out to their houses a few times a year, but for someone living 6.2 miles across the bridge, forget it. They're on their own. But even with the use of a third family car, Elizabeth has other worries.

Gentle-hearted and soft-spoken normally, Beth grins at the news of our winning the bid as we make sugar cookies in the old kitchen one afternoon approaching Halloween. Watching her pound on the dough with the rolling pin, however, I suspect there is more grimace than grin to her face. "I'm used to this old house," she says as she selects a heart-shaped cookie cutter, her favorite. "When I come in at night and go upstairs in this old house, I know I'm at the top even in the dark because of the creak in the step. There's no claw-foot tub at that Frentress place either," she reminds me, hammering down on the word "Frentress."

There's no denying that our old brick Federalist house has charm, but I'd always believed it was wasted on children who prefer modern houses like their friends have, ones with finished basement family rooms and fiberglass tub-shower units. Suddenly Elizabeth now sounds like *This Old House* guru Bob Villa talking about "the historically significant limestone cellar" and the "authentic built-in leaded glass cabinetry." When it comes down to it, Elizabeth is a traditionalist who doesn't favor change. "I know it's your dream," she finally acknowledges, selecting another cookie cutter, this time a witch, "but that river house is my nightmare." She guillotines the dough with the cutter.

Even scraping off layer after layer of wallpaper doesn't compare to negotiating Elizabeth's comfort with the move. As exhausted as we are by hours of prying loose the molded woodwork and sanding walls, Jerry and I lay in bed a few nights after the cookie-chopping conversation, our eyes wide open, staring at the ceiling. He is the first to speak: "How are we going to help Elizabeth with the move?"

She's easy-going. Beth has never been a demanding person, except when it really matters to her. Dismissing her resistance is not even on the farthest edges of our parental radar. Realizing that she loves the old house more because of pleasant family events and holidays than because of its horsehair plaster and hardwood floors, we begin constructing a series of new events to make the Frentress house become home.

As Jerry drifts off, I think long into the darkness about Elizabeth. She is at a crucial stage, standing up for herself, deciding where her loyalties are, and determining the kind of woman she's becoming. I do not wish to divert her natural tendencies any more than I do the river's. Yet I know with certainty that change will contribute to who she becomes, to how she will manage her future, to how she will keep herself bending like a reed rather than breaking like a stick.

"Begin where she is," I recall from education psychology classes back in my undergraduate years. I plan weekly family pizza parties at Frentress. And her room, I think to myself, she should have her way with her room—metalicized wall paint so she can stick posters and photos to it (as well as those magnets from Strawberry Point, Iowa, her new favorite town). Parties, I muse further—she could have all her friends to the lake this spring.

Our "Call of the Wild" girl, the only one to volunteer to go out on that first trip on the river on April 1 of each year, Elizabeth, I hope, will mainly be won over by the river itself.

Because we're renovating, the heat and electricity are shut off. Beth, Andrew, and James join Jerry and me around the glass patio table brought into the rubble of the front room at Frentress the following Sunday, their teeth chattering as their breath condenses in clouds in the chilly air. The weather had turned colder and, as it often does in the Midwest in late fall, dropped thirty-five degrees overnight.

Huddling in sweaters and heavy woolen coats, Jerry and I force grins at the three children sitting around the table with us. They do not respond in kind, perhaps because their jaws are frozen. We set logs and sticks ablaze in the fireplace, but it doesn't do much to warm the room or their moods. They seem more interested in finding ways to eat Tugboat Willy's pizza without removing their woolen gloves than in the pleasantries we are hoping to foster.

"What are you going to be for Halloween?" is my first paltry effort to get them talking. Obviously too old for trick-or-treating, they'd normally laugh at this question and then toss out outlandish ideas. Elizabeth, at five-foot-ten, for example, might say, "I think I'll be a munchkin." James, training for singing opera, might decide, "I'll be Barry Manilow" and he'd rip out, "Her name was Lola, she was a showgirl" from "Copacabana"; and Andrew could suggest he'd become "Recycle Man," wearing all the paper bags in the house as his costume. Instead, their grim reply comes nearly in unison, "Haven't thought about it." Next, I ask who needs new skates in order to skate on the lake this winter. There's silence as they pick cheese and pepperonis off the pizza in front of them. Finally, when I ask where we are on the dead mouse count, Mr. Numbers, James, at least groans a response, "Fifteen."

Ironically, Elizabeth is the first to speak up, "Can Bobby come over here next week?" Her current boyfriend lives south along the river in Bellevue. "Sure, have him meet us here for pizza next Sunday." I'm eager to have him join us because he's always got interesting stories to tell about peculiar happenings in Bellevue. He's also a river rat, and the potential for him to positively influence Beth when it comes to her attitude about the river house doesn't escape me.

During the weeks ahead, while Jerry, Josh, and I rebuild the interior of the house, our children's friends drop by. Not only Bobby, but also Ian, Natalie, Dan, Curt, Sara, Anna, and Tim show up. As I see the steady stream of them coming by, it occurs to me that our children have invited them in an attempt to christen the place with friends.

I am amazed by how comfortable they are despite the conditions of the house: carpetless down to the plywood underlayment, nails protruding from walls and woodwork, plaster dust in the air, saw-horses, staple guns, and circular saws everywhere. The young people build bonfires and roast marshmallows on the beach outside. In early December, after three days of hard freeze, they join us shoveling snow off the lake to fashion a skating area. I know that even Elizabeth is on a journey moving toward accepting the river house the day she asks, "When does the phone come in?"

As I skate on the river for the first time, I realize this is the kind of moment that will grow more intense over the years, almost stronger in memory than in the present living of it. Back when I was eight, I considered ice a funny trick of nature, because liquid was overcome by the frozen form of itself. When Sister John Mary said walking on water was a miracle, I knew better. I walked on water every time I set my skate-clad foot on the pond. Always a Midwesterner at heart, I am invigorated by temperatures below thirty-two degrees. I love seeing my own breath condense into puffs as I talk, my spoken words becoming visible in the air.

But I haven't skated in at least fifteen years. I am determined but hesitant. I'm not as young as I was back then, and the years have not been any kinder to my old white figure skates; the leather is dried and cracked, the once-silver blades dulled to gray. I used to glide around the rink over in Iowa, teaching our kids to skate when they were little. Once they had tired and needed to rest by sipping hot chocolate, I loved nothing better than to leave them with Jerry and take off on the rink on my own.

On those afternoons years ago, with Jerry and the kids thawing in the warming house, I'd head down and approach the ice, pick in to get a firm start, and push off with long smooth glides around the circumference. Three or four times around and I was up to speed. I delighted in twists and turns on the ice, figure eights, and skating backward. There's something in the rhythm of it—the way my arms swing, nearly flapping, syncopating the glide, glide, glide of my legs. I find skating is as close as I'll ever get to flying. It is not the speed that attracts me but the seamlessness of motion, of my arms and legs working with such easy precision.

But my old skates have become so stiff that they will not yield to my foot. Jerry watches as I grow frustrated, attempting to weave laces through rusted eyelets. At breakfast, he gives me an early birthday card with a coupon for new skates inside. Remembering that

Andrew last went skating years before he grew into size tens, I invite him along to Kunnert Sports early that afternoon.

As I gaze upon the rows of bladed boots, I am pleased that the technology of ice skates has not changed. "Figure and Hockey are still the two common categories," the saleswoman tells us. There are a few upscale pairs in dark purple and orange, of course, but overall the array looks very much like it did when I was eight, flying across those childhood ponds. Andrew taps the counter impatiently as the woman sharpens his blades. He taps faster as she tells him her own stories of growing up at Frentress and skating the lake. He is out the door before the woman even gets mine out of the box.

Once more at the lake, Andrew and I race each other from the car through the backyard and down to the beach. A stream of water separates us from thin ice, and it's another three or four feet to solid ice. Walking out on the neighbors' dock embedded in the hardened river, I sit with my legs dangling over the edge as I lace up. Andrew is already on his feet and ready to go. I watch him take off with the slant of the late afternoon sun streaking through his hair, and I wonder if I have ever seen him happier than he is right now. Although tracks on the surface testify that four-wheelers have been out on this crystal lake earlier in the day, just now it is only the two of us.

I skated Lake Michigan as a child, but it was rough going with water that froze in the shape of waves and with rocks bubbling up to wart the surface. This backwater slough, however, is smooth and more transparent in its frozen state than I have ever seen the river in July. There's been only a trace of snow, which melted yesterday, so we have a vast field of ice.

Andrew is the first to find a leaf frozen into the ice. Minutes later, investigating something shiny on the surface, I spot a three-inch fish caught in midswim by the quick freeze of the preceding week. We are visual scavengers, Andrew and I, cataloging a quarter, a Coke can, a life ring, all things that two weeks ago floated beneath the surface but that now appear like found items in a frieze panel one might see at the art gallery.

"What are you staring at?" Elizabeth's voice breaks through our collectors' reverie. I stand up, knowing I will never be able to explain to a sixteen-year-old why I am staring down into the frozen river delighted by finding a pop tab down there. She sets six ceramic mugs and a canteen of hot chocolate down on the dock, "Thought you might need this about now." Andrew and I join her on the dock drinking hot chocolate. Before long, Jason and his girlfriend, Carrie, show up, too. They are visiting for the day. Jerry arrives, his old black skates slung over his shoulder.

The afternoon sun descends lower with every sip. Beth looks over her cup at Andrew, and her eyes take on a mischief I've seen before: "Bet you can't pull me across the lake on the saucer!" Although both of them tower over me, for this one afternoon, they are little kids again, her sitting cross-legged in the saucer yelling, "Mush, mush!" as Andrew twirls her in arcs around the ice toward the island across the way. Jason and Carrie join in as well, after pelting one another with snowballs.

I recall once when Andrew was five and had had quite enough of his four overbearing siblings. One afternoon, he stomped his foot and declared emphatically, "You are NOT the bosses of me!" Now, here he is, nearly as tall as Beth, pulling her around the lake. Jerry promises to watch over them just in case the ice isn't uniformly thick, and I take the opportunity to skate up the lake toward the cut to the main channel.

The river will freeze all the way out on the main channel eventually, but for now it's too early in the season. I'd seen the main channel still streaming fluid, open water, as we crossed the bridge coming from Kunnert's this afternoon.

In summer, I have to watch the current to read the water for wing dams and stump fields. That telltale line of water folding back upon itself, usually running from a pointed red "nun" buoy to the tip of an island, is warning enough of an underwater stone wall. Fast current, too, reminds me to proceed cautiously when entering the lock chamber, thus avoiding smashing into the concrete wall.

But now, even in winter, I'm finding I have to be aware of the current. Because the current is often swifter at the cut connecting the main channel to backwaters, those cuts are slower to freeze. Up ahead, the cut is still a lane of open water surrounded by ice. Of course, before I'd actually hit water, I'll be skating on very thin ice.

Taking long glides on the ice, I am a quarter mile up the lake in no time. With most of the cottages packed up for the winter, it's strangely still now, but the stillness makes me even more aware of my own movement on the ice. My skates are gleaming golden in the sun, I am sure. With my arms raised to cross an imaginary finish line, I am Hans Brinker, the graceful skater whose movements on ice bring to mind Fred Astaire and Ginger Rogers.

Skating now as if I were eight again, I feel myself letting go. The cares and hesitancies of being a grown woman, of worrying about breaking a bone or appearing foolish, on this birthday when I've received my AARP card, disappear with every stroke as I make my way farther up the shoreline. The challenges of renovating the house, of future floods, of the children's worries, and of juggling too much to do in too little time melt away for the time being.

Without a doubt, this is the biggest pond I have ever skated. To go so far without having to turn around makes me hum and then yodel. If Elizabeth were in range, she'd cringe to hear me finally sing "Black Water" by the Doobie Brothers—"Mississippi moon, won't you keep on shinin' on me?"—but she and Andrew are too far to hear. I sing even louder, dancing on my picks as I do. Sure enough, the cut out to the main channel is still watery. A lone bald eagle circles overhead, probably hunting for any last shad.

To avoid thin ice at the cut ahead, I turn back reluctantly. I glide across to the other side of the slough. Skating across the biggest river in the country is a heady experience. I think back to last winter when I waited, waited, waited to get back out on the river in April. This year will be different. I am on the river *now*, after all, and it's only December.

By the time I approach Elizabeth, Andrew, Jason, and Carrie— now making snow angels on the ice—I am flying. It is the sensation of taking wing, not one of racing, that I celebrate. Pure freedom. And then the only possible partner eagle to my soaring, Jerry shows up to skate the final yards of the lake with me hand in hand.

That night, back up the hill at our old house in town, after dinner is cleared away, family members drift back to activities of their own. Jason and Carrie have gone back to jobs in Iowa City. James, Elizabeth, and Andrew are off doing homework, attending practice, and working. Jerry leaves to work out at the Loras College indoor pool. Having skated all afternoon, I opt out of joining him. I have this old brick Federalist house to myself.

With a toasty fire radiating after the exercise of the afternoon, I decide my composition students' papers can wait one more day before grading. I sit rocking somewhere between sleep and wakefulness. Something as simple as a huge pond of frozen water has given me peace today. The chilly but soft breeze through the needles of the pines whispers to me yet.

I reflect on the Mississippi, on how it means more to me than just a place to recreate. Skating and boating on it are enjoyable, of course, but nature moves me beyond amusement. There have been quasi-successful efforts to control the Mississippi, but in spite of them all, the river still rises and falls, freezes and melts of its own accord, beyond human control.

We'll renovate the house, take out walls, erect new ones, move pipes, install heat, and the like. We'll fix the waterfront, too, probably with rip-rap rocks. But I won't ever renovate the river. Even if I tried, I'd fail. It is this fact—the river's hugeness, its devious power, its ability to exist with or without me—that gives me such peace. The Mississippi will always be in charge, claiming forcefully, *You are not the boss of me.*

Through my half-closed eyelids, I see more clearly than I have seen in the months of worry over bidding and winning, cleaning and remodeling. I see clear through ahead to early spring. The great blue herons have returned to the creek running alongside our new house. The lone bald eagle I spotted this afternoon will be joined by hundreds of others on our back slough lake for one last meal before they head up north for nesting. And my own wild birds— James, Elizabeth, Andrew, Jason, and Rebekah—will return to our new nest to join in a family float, with their rafts and lifesaver rings tethered to the dock. Even Beth will be smiling.

I imagine Jerry and me upstairs sitting on the veranda outside our bedroom overlooking the river. In my vision, the beach is submerged several feet under the spring rise, but high water won't last forever. We chat about the full moon the night before, casting its oval disk reflection onto the lake as we fell asleep.

As I continue to rock by the fireplace here in our old Federalist house, I can almost hear the river running through the basement of the river house. All the same, in my vision, Jerry and I toast one another and then turn to toast the Mississippi. I am sure I see the river raise a wave in return.

But I quickly discharge that last thought as I lean forward to stoke the dying embers. The Mississippi does not love me. No person can ever hope to take ownership of something as wild as the Mississippi. Yes, it is a river that connects my life, that marks the seasons of change, but, no, it is not *my* river. If there is any possession to be had, certainly it is the river's. For better or worse, it is a river that runs through *me*.

Critters

We moved into the limestone house at Frentress Lake in May. I'm finally again living on water years after leaving Lake Michigan. Months of cleaning and remodeling had brought us to loggerheads at times. One whole day went to disagreeing about which refrigerator would best tolerate being tipped on its side to be raised up on sawhorses when rising waters threatened the first floor. Two entire afternoons were wasted on arguing which kitchen cabinets were best. A week was spent consternating over which commode to install—the taller, more comfortable ADA one, or just a regular stool? But now that's all over. Well, nearly over. There's still no woodwork trim on the first floor, the front riverbank needs bolstering, and there's varnishing yet to be done—and who needs a door on the bathroom, anyway?

Even though we weren't living here full-time until May, daily trips to work on the house provided a peek at what we'd gotten ourselves into.

Five months before we moved in, on a Saturday when Jerry and I had come to paint the living room, I was startled to find trucks and trailers parked all over our backyard. Through the front glass patio doors, I spotted more than thirty snowmobiles on the ice surrounding our dock. Maybe it was the contents of all those coolers they'd hauled out on the ice that made them forget about private property. The thrill of speeding back and forth across the ice, at nine million miles an hour, back and forth, back and forth, eludes me still. Jack, a county board member who lives up the road, tells me that because the lake is public property, there's not a legal thing we can do about those snowmobiles. In addition to interior renovation, we began planning exterior installation of No Trespassing signs.

Three months before we moved in, I was greeted by one of the residents as I pulled onto the gravel road, "Osty's plane went through the ice." That was sobering—not even Steve Osterberger, an expert pilot, could have guessed the ice would break through in February. There were four-wheelers, ice boats, and men and women with ropes trying to heave the sea plane out of the hole in the frozen lake. At dusk I had to leave, but like other residents, I turned on lakeside lights to assist in the rescue. I'll never understand how he got that plane out, but there he was three months later flying the perimeter of the lake the day we moved in.

Two months before we moved in, startled by what I saw, I dropped a boxload of doorknobs and hinges on the sidewalk as I carried them in from the car. In the trees surrounding our house, I counted sixty-two American bald eagles. With the weather warming, they were feasting on gizzard shad showing up in the thin stream melting along the shoreline. Sixty-two!

Six weeks before we moved in, Jerry and I paddled a canoe around the perimeter of the lake, dodging ice floes with every stroke of the paddles. With temperatures occasionally in the sixties, the ice had broken up. Once again, we had open water all the way across the lake. At the tip of the lake, we thought we'd spotted a backwater scavenger's delight, two big floats we might use under our dock, but they turned out to be waterlogged, deflated pontoons and driftwood. Because they were embedded in hundreds of dead fish, we left these treasure chests for others more desperate than we were.

Four weeks before we moved in, the river's edge reeked of thousands of dead fish. Most were about six inches long, but every so often, I'd come across a big fat aromatic one. Standing on the dock, Andrew and his friend Ian tried to sink them with rocks and swirl them around with boat oars. Who'd have thought a carpet of dead fish could be so much fun. It was fun and frolic for the gulls, too.

If it came to a showdown of cacophony between the birds of Frentress Lake and the birds in Alfred Hitchcock's famous thriller, our gulls would win, beaks down. Clearing the yard of brush and fish heads dropped by the birds one afternoon, I heard a neighbor's rifle go off. He wasn't trying to kill the gulls. In fact, he'd shot into

A lone bald eagle soars over the Mississippi.
Telegraph Herald, *Dubuque, Iowa*

the air *away* from the lake just to scare them off to get some peace and quiet. All the gulls flew off, but the promise of thousands of shad eyes was too delicious to deny, and they were back within fifteen minutes.

Two weeks before we moved in, I drove our son James to Europe. Not Europe exactly, but to Chicago's O'Hare Airport so Lufthansa could deliver him to Munich. In nearby Prien, he studied German. He'd also charted out a plan to Eurail it to twenty-seven operas in Italy, England, France, and Austria in addition to German performances.

It felt peculiar to move into a new house without James. It was even odder to talk to him on the phone, his voice sounding as if he was on the island just across the lake as I stood out on the front deck, watching seagulls. One day he called to share his good luck. He'd discovered that the sewers near the Bayerische Staatsoper opera house had unintentionally been constructed in such a way that you could stand on the sidewalk and hear *Pique Dame* for free rising up from beneath the street. As I pictured him there along the streets of Munich, his ear turned to the lovely tones of Placido Domingo emanating from the concrete, I saw a fish leap up out of the surface of the Mississippi.

Although our adult children, Bekah and Jason, have been living in households of their own for years now and are joined by spouses and a son each (the amazing rhyming cousins, Quin and Finn), it feels peculiar to move into a new house without them as well. Having made all our other house moves with these two oldest, their absence in this one is more noticeable than one might have guessed.

One week before we moved, I turned in final grades for my college students. Afterward, driving up the Lake Road, I stopped at Fincel's for just-picked asparagus and tomatoes for dinner. The Fincel family vegetable farm is best known in these regions for the sweetest corn in the heartland. It's so fine that folks have been known to ship it to New York for wedding dinners.

The week we moved in, with Beth and Andrew still in school and Jerry off at work, I settled in at the river with the place all to myself during the day. Then, before the summer season had started, there weren't many residents in the region.

Lucky, our beagle, kept me company on long walks through the back woods surrounding the lake. She was keen after every rabbit. Nature called her so strongly that she nearly ran into the river before remembering that she hates water. Since adopting her from the Humane Society shelter two years ago, we've tried to convince her that she comes from a proud breed of hunting dogs who regularly dove into wild waters after game, but in May, she'd still leap over the smallest of rain puddles to avoid getting wet.

When I'd run into city folks asking, "What's it like living over there?" I struggled with the semantics of our new place. I still do. Saying "cottage at Frentress" can refer to residences varying from humble rustic cabins to expensive three-level chalets with Jacuzzis. Mostly, the label *cottage* is determined not by the structure but by the habits of the residents. If you're here for summer only, yours is a cottage. Once our neighbors realize we're here to stay, they'll refer to our place as a "house."

There are roughly thirty-five houses and cottages along this back slough. The inhabitants include a banker, two high school teachers, a real estate agent, a nurse, a haberdasher, two construction workers, a concert pianist, a dentist, a professional Santa Claus and Mrs. Claus, a couple of industrialists, a downhill ski instructor, a retired football coach, a vegetable farmer, an airline pilot, several full-time parents, a furniture salesman, two secretaries, two county board members (from both sides of the river), a bookkeeper, several enterprising cooks, a highway operations specialist, a child caregiver, a matriarch, a museum director, and me.

We could nearly exist on our own if we had to. There are no lawyers, but then we'd be unlikely to sue one another anyway. There's only one plumber, but given our chief source of water problems, more than one plumber wouldn't be all that useful. I suppose as a writer, I'm about the most useless resident in the neighborhood. True, I've got that 1850s cast-iron circular knitter in the corner, which can crank out a pair of wool socks in an hour. Then, too, someone has to write the obituaries and eulogies. Maybe they'll let me stay after all.

Once the summer people returned, I got to know folks, and I appreciated afresh how the river attracts all kinds. Gini came knocking one afternoon. Peering through the window and seeing Jerry resting on the sofa, she rapped even more loudly. She wanted to see what we had "done with the place." I came to realize that whenever I want to stir community involvement here along the river, Gini's the person to call first. She reminds me of sunlight reflecting like diamonds on the river at high noon, all sunnysparks and energy. Following her, there was a steady stream of neighbors tapping at the doors wanting a look-see.

Dick never came rapping, but I met him one afternoon over mutual bonfires. He winters in Texas, but like the herons nesting over the creek between our two houses, he can't wait to return to the river as soon as the ice breaks up. When I ask him how long he'd stay up north, he smiles. "If it snows tomorrow, I'll leave tonight," he responds as he leans on his shovel. He is out digging a trench to keep the side creek open to the river, thus keeping a steady overturn of water. Dick's retired, and he'll tell you that his only job is to hang out on the dock and keep a lookout on our end of the slough, "I'm sort of a river caretaker."

I spot him one morning eyeing the dead tree near the beach. We'd tried to burn it down last winter but didn't build enough bonfires.

"I'll pull that tree out for you," he offers. His son-in-law, Gary, also retired, joins him daily at his dock. Two weeks later, as I sit on the front deck drinking coffee one morning, I see Dick and Gary back their pickup to that tree, attach chains, and topple it.

Once in a while, I see Dick motor off early in the morning toward the far end of the lake. "Gone fishin'," he reports, or "Just clearing debris." He hauls fallen timber to the top of the pond where beavers make good use of it. Just last week, he and Gary took a load of rail- road ties that had shored up on the beach to a woman up the road who needed a retaining wall for her yard. "She's tight on funds," they explained, and these would be free materials.

Watching him as he watches twilight on a near nightly schedule, I realize Dick has landed the good life. I worry a bit, however, when Andrew as a teenager tells me that this is the life he aspires to, sitting around the docks and "being retired."

"When the river gets to fifteen feet, it'll be in your basement," Dick warns a few weeks after we move in. I tune in to daily Corps of Engineers river stage predictions on the Internet. The day before it is supposed to rise to fifteen feet, Jerry and I head down to the basement and, under a full moon, open the double glass doors. As we look at those muddy waters edging up the lawn, I whisper, "Come on in, Mississippi."

There's something wondrously romantic and sensual about that night. To invite the greatest river in America to run through the foundation of our house makes me quiver yet. For three weeks, I fall asleep at night to thump, thump, thumping from the basement as two feet of water knocks the wheelbarrow against the cinder block wall. I come to consider it my own personal symphony. A few seasons from now, I imagine, the romance will wear off, but this summer, I even welcome fish flies, those black beauties that swarm in for twenty-four hours and then die, their carcasses blan- keting the lawn.

It was an unusually long season of high water on the upper river. We couldn't even get the boat in the water until late June. For the first time in all my years on the Mississippi, as a fellow dock owner, I sympathize with Arnie over at the Midtown Marina boat shop. I can well imagine angry slip renters throughout May tapping their fingers at his chest, demanding those boats be put in the water. Even once the river recedes, we still have barely any beach compared to the previous year's low-water stage. But I'm not complaining. Our living room stayed dry, and there is no silt to shovel out the front door.

Our adult children return more frequently once we move onto the river. Married happily, Bekah's life is more settled than last year. Too, Jason had finished college and is headed on to law school, so they are both in more of a position to visit than they'd been for a while. All the same, I can't help but believe that the river itself calls to them. Lounging on tubes and rafts, eight of us latched on to one another's flotation devices one steamy afternoon following a week of temperatures in the upper nineties. With Andrew, Elizabeth, Jason, Jerry, Bekah, and me alongside son-in-law Jerod and Jason's fiancée, Carrie, we have our own flotilla out there.

Although I find the world changes more rapidly than a fisher rebaiting her hook by a wing dam, the July Fourth Frentress parade could have marched right out of my memories of the 1950s. "The Stone Age. The era of one-room schoolhouses," James would claim about my childhood days when I lived in a small lake village. Back then, it was the kind of place where you didn't have to lock your doors at night or your cars at any time. Our parades had no expensive costumes, no spectator sites marked off by yellow safety tape, and no buses to transport people from their cars to the parade area. The parades of my youth were simple, straightforward, and homemade.

Ruth had warned me, back when we were bidding on the house, that none of the residents are spectators at the parade because everyone is in it. Gini shows up at the door observing that with the tall people in our family, surely we can provide the Abe Lincoln?

James is off in Germany visiting Mad King Ludwig's castle. Andrew won't don the homemade curly brown yarn beard to save his life. Elizabeth is tall but puts the matter to rest: "I'm not *that* much of a feminist." Jason is unanimously voted into office for the day.

We sit in the back of a pony cart with him as he tips his stovepipe hat, a back cardboard tube we'd created out of someone's recycled craft project. I wear a red, white, and blue five-pointed star headdress. Tiny lights on the end of each point flash as I sit next to Abe. Andrew has tied a red, white, and blue ribbon to Lucky's collar and marches her alongside the cart. Elizabeth somehow manages to escape by volunteering to work at the historical society's ice cream social across the bridge in Iowa. I'll get her involved next year, I plot.

Even though it's a typically hot midwestern July Fourth, it still won't get the better of our neighbor Rod. He'd flown in from his other home in California the week before. He comes to the parade prepared. If you grow thirsty, all you have to do is nod in Rod's direction. He drives over to your parade spot in his tractor, lowers the backhoe, and offers you an icy can of soda or beer right out of the loader.

If you'd happened upon the parade without prior explanation, you might mistake it for Halloween festivities. There are horses with cowboys on their backs, seven-year-old astronauts wrapped in tinfoil space suits, politically incorrect kids wearing war paint sitting in a canoe atop a trailer, clowns, and Rita as drum majorette. Ben Graham and his wife had a baby this year, so Ben has donned a diaper as his costume. As empress of the parade, Gini is devastating in her bright red toga, sparkly earrings, and irresistible smile, urging everyone to take time to actually celebrate the day. Completing the scene, Steve Osterberger flys overhead in his resurrected sea plane.

The parade route stretched all of four blocks, from one end of the lake road to the other. Ruth brings up the rear with her little red wagon and sign reading, "The End." The parade culminates in a potluck across the back lawns—lawns free of fences and gates. And there's always root-beer floats. Dining on hot dogs, Fincel's corn on the cob, and green Jell-O salad across the table from Ruth and Joe, I come to realize how important this event is to those who live here. Like other residents, Ruth is already saying, "Next year, let's..."

Lucky, too, celebrates a sort of Independence Day of her own when my friend and I take her out on her pontoon boat the following week. We load up Sue's grandkids along with Andrew and Lucky. We motor across the channel, and as we sit on Nine-Mile Island looking out over the horizon beyond our knitting needles, something catches my ear, a thwacking underwater sound. I look to the beach expecting that I've dropped the ball of yarn again, but it sits safely in my bag. It turns out a few dozen clamshells were glistening in the sun, and curiosity had gotten the better of Lucky's fear. She was standing with all four feet in water, pawing away at the shells. She isn't completely liberated from her hatred of water, however, and she still always leaps over tiny puddles along our daily walks. But if you toss a handful of shells into the river, she dives in like a real beagle. She won the household's July river rat of the month award.

Although some of the doors still need varnishing and there is yet a spot to patch in the back room, the house feels finished when James returns in August. James likes the river well enough, but he isn't particularly enthused with the great outdoors. Nonetheless, he achieved top August river rat status one morning shortly after his arrival home.

There'd been one boat that persisted in dropping anchor just a few feet from our dock. On this particular morning, the scantily clad young couple were dancing on board as they smoked cigarettes, the rancid Marlboro fog wafting in through our front screens. "It's bad enough they come so close," James commented, "but worse is that music!" After three months of filling his ears with Bryn Terfel, Hei-Kyung Hong, and "Die Walküre," he couldn't abide the combination of bubblegum tunes laced with twangy rhyming lyrics.

"Watch this," he grinned, heading out on the veranda overlooking the river. Like a pitcher readying his arm for the game, James warmed up by singing a few scales, his voice booming out over the water. Then he broke into full aria from the *Marriage of Figaro* in deep, bellowing bass tones. Within seconds, the boaters pulled up anchor and tore away. "Who says opera doesn't have practical application?" James laughed. If he's gone again next summer, I'll have to invest in an outdoor speaker system and a collection of Pavarotti CDs. I wonder how snowmobilers feel about opera?

As much as James chases off intruders, Andrew courts them. Finding an empty aquarium at the back of one of the closets, he places it on the front deck. For a few weeks, this tank is home to water bugs, two frogs, a snake, worms, and several other slimy creatures he collects. By September, however, Andrew is also developing into his own form of full river rat–hood, appreciative that along the shore, we're the outsiders. If anyone should be in a tank, it shouldn't be the frogs, he decides, and sets his captives free just as the sun dips beneath the treeline on the west side of the lake.

Andrew's benevolence toward critters takes me back to earlier years, when his oldest sibling, Rebekah, was two. "What shall we name him?" I'd asked her about the fly that had landed on her arm. As an anti-capital-punishment, pro-gun-control pacifist, I wanted to inculcate in her a respect for life, even life as insignificant as a housefly. (I also wanted to quiet her screaming.) "Albert," she'd decided. To this day, she can't swat a fly without asking forgiveness from "Albert."

Living on the backwaters, I hear nature knocking at every turn. There are two great blue herons living in nests over the creek at the side of our property. Gone for the winter, they showed up this spring about a month before we moved in. It's probably not the same pair, but they look familiar all the same.

Although I've encountered herons before, I've never had one roosting on my front deck. Dick tells me there have been herons nesting in the treetops here for as far back as he remembers. Although they swoop and soar in perfect unison, their six-foot wing-spans reflecting the sun, they hunt alone. Observing one in pursuit of its next meal reminds me of watching a child stealing the last cookie off a plate when she's sure no one sees.

The bird stands motionless except for its eyes darting about to locate fish, mice, small birds, and frogs. At first extending its neck when a meal trots, hops, or swims by, the bird slowly pulls its neck back into the curved shape of a question mark. It stealthily moves one leg toward the prey. Then, lightning fast, the great blue's bill is in the water—the bird flings dinner into the air and swallows it in one deft movement, dropping that frog headfirst down its gullet.

Herons have a sensible way of sharing the duties of parenting, too. During incubation, the male sits on the nest by day, and the female takes her turn at night. After the eggs hatch, the pair continues the schedule, each taking a shift feeding and watching over the brood. I'm told that great blues usually nest in colonies, but the most I ever see along the side creek are two. Non-river friends mistake the great blue for cranes, but when you see them in the air, there's no comparison. A crane flies with its neck straight forward. The heron pulls its neck in between its shoulders into the shape of a tight *S*. Somewhat gawky in appearance on land, there's nothing as graceful as a great blue in flight. I can nearly feel the air around it swish against the flapping of wings.

A lone muskrat swims along backwater shores.

There are laws against hunting on our side of the lake as well as on the island preserve directly across from us. But farther downstream, it's open season on ducks and other birds. I watch flatboats topped with twig and grass blinds. They're loaded with guns and camouflaged hunters as they zoom farther back in the slough. Within minutes, the unmistakable sound of gunfire shatters the air.

As one who eats meat, I can't ethically object when the main mission of hunting is to bring home dinner—even if I don't want to be the one to pull the trigger. But something about killing being a sport sticks in my craw. When I read interviews with young boys and girls exhilarated by counting the points of their dead bucks, the bravado grates on me. Kids shouldn't be reveling in killing animals any more than they should be in wiping out enemies on video games or going to war to kill other people in hope of winning one for the Gipper.

State conservation departments often seem increasingly interested in promoting the "bullets 'n hooks" aspect of their mission and relegate to second position "living off the land" or simply enjoying the beauty of nature. I appreciate nature's call to humans to provide for our own food sources directly. I understand a reluctance to depend upon the ever-growing corporate mechanization of food production and the wish to avoid the preservatives and chemicals needed to enhance shelf life. As much as the vegetable gardener yearns for her own fresh tomatoes, some fishers and hunters also hunger for a more direct connection to meat sources. When I consider how far the plastic-wrapped packages in supermarkets are from the natural world of edibles, I have to admit that at their best, hunting and fishing keep us real about what we eat and where it comes from.

Certainly, animals and plants die in order to sustain other members of the food chain. When our golden retriever Corkie "gifted" us with eyeless dead fish on the doorstep and the rent limbs of a bloodied baby rabbit scattered across our living room rug, our children ran screaming from the room. They'd come to think of their beloved Corkie as a civilized human sister. Her natural canine behavior seemed barbarian to them. I taught them about how life sustains other life through death and how this assists in achieving the ecological balance of the planet. I think I even quoted Aldo Leopold's "Thinking Like a Mountain." (Try explaining to an eight-year-old that we're not always at the top of the food chain.) But imagine if the kids and I had danced to celebrate Corkie's kill. What if we'd had the baby rabbit stuffed and mounted for display in a trophy case, a proud declaration of her prowess. It doesn't make any more sense to me in the human world than it does in the realm of canines.

It's the culture of killing, the reveling in the sport of it, that disturbs me. In a part of the country that thrives upon planting, growing, and nurturing corn and soybean, it seems downright anti-midwestern to have plaques and prizes for killing something— almost anything—as long as it is huge or heavy.

Not too long ago, however, the hunters and fishers of Frentress Lake and I found ourselves on the same side of the ecological fence. They joined me one morning at the river house to collaborate about an upcoming Corps meeting regarding Army Corps of Engineers proposals to extend locks. The hunters and fishers were motivated by preserving and restoring habitat so there would be fish and wildlife to supply their dinner tables. I was motivated by the loss of wetlands and wishes for the restored health of the river. Theirs was a particularly enlightened view and I gained new respect for those who hunt and fish in order to enjoy nature—rather than to hang a trophy over the fireplace.

Tonight, though, Jerry is out of town, the kids are off-premises, and not even a mouse is stirring. I've taken shelter in the house to get away from mosquitoes and fish flies. They're thick out there, so I've turned off all but one spotlight—to assist wayward boaters through the night. For the heck of it, I've been doodling with words on paper. My sole semantic discovery is that if only a few letters are subtracted from my first and last names, I'm KatFish. Pleased with my wordplay, I stare out at the river through the front windows.

In this misty Mississippi River night, I discover a tree frog on the outside of the patio doors shimmying up the glass pane. There are bats dive-bombing for insects in our spotlight beams outside. Out there, too, fish flies join the tree frog, landing on the panes until they nearly blanket one side of the house. As I see the outdoor life filling up around me, I am reminded of how small I really am, of my tiny place in the river's vast universe.

I stare at the frog's underbody against the glass. I'm surrounded by four enormous double-paned doors and several even more enormous glass windows, and the awareness grows on me slowly at first. In a flash, I have the eerie sensation that the tree frog is studying its captured critter—counting appendages, wondering about its eating habits, and searching for wings. Now, as the frog's critter, one female *Homo sapiens*, I find my glass house transformed. I am on the inside looking out of a huge human aquarium.

Gulf

Like Louisiana levees, my heart breaks for New Orleans, Mississippi, and all areas rammed by the hurricanes of 2005. That late August evening, as America waited in awestruck fear for Katrina to hit the Gulf Coast full force at category five, I found myself alone at home. Andrew was overnight at Ian's house, James had gone out with friends, and Elizabeth had recently returned to college in Madison for the fall term. Jerry was attending a White House Conference on Cooperative Conservation in St. Louis, which, ironically enough, promoted conservation by giving land over to ranchers. Many of the specially invited environmentalists boycotted.

Although I knew my oldest two adult children were far from hurricane paths, I called them anyway to make sure. I caught Jason, wife Carrie, and toddler Finn just returning to their apartment in Washington, D.C., from visiting the National Zoo. I could hear Finn roaring like a lion in the background. Jason and Carrie sounded exhilarated by a day spent with their own offspring version of Huckleberry Finn, so I was assured that everything their way was settled. I found Bekah and husband Jerod at home playing Chase-the-Bear with three-year-old Quin: "We had to turn off the news, Mom. Quin got frightened." Her voice was replaced by Quin's: "It's okay, Granny Kate. Mommy and Pop will keep us safe."

Relishing how parents can envelop a child's fears until he feels carefree once more, I put the phone down and returned to the den, where television news reminded me that no one could put their arms around Mississippi and Louisiana tonight to chase away this giant boogey man. Secure within the safety of my own home, far from flood season on the Upper Mississippi, I poured myself into caring about those in the path of Katrina. I tried to keep the watch with our downriver neighbors through the night, but I dozed off restlessly in the armchair to the sounds of CNN predictions and windblown reporters.

By morning, news sources reported that Katrina was only a category three, and New Orleans had once again "dodged a bullet." Everyone knows what they meant by "bullet": Any city below sea level, sooner or later, will be hit by the Big One, and the results would be devastating.

In the days following, however, my spirit sank as images of rising Lake Pontchartrain and Gulf waters surged into the city, overtopping levees a second time. National Public Radio interviews with those fetched from rooftops left me feeling abandoned by my own inability to sufficiently help this sister city to the south. Evacuation footage revealed well-to-do people traveling north in SUVs with empty seats. The promised safe haven of the Superdome turned into hell, leaving people victims of unspeakable filth, crime, and even death. Even Geraldo Rivera temporarily gained respectability when he hoisted a toddler up to cameras urging that FOX News get beyond political agendas and see the horror growing worse by the second.

The whole world saw the aftermath play out on television screens, but the organizations and agencies expert in such disaster management failed to show up for several days. As an excuse, some claimed the news media was exaggerating. Others claimed, "We didn't realize how bad it was." Parking lots full of buses immobilized by red tape failed to carry thousands more to safety. Nursing home residents died needlessly. These images still plague me, months after Katrina. They probably always will.

This is America, I thought to myself. This can't be happening here.

I used to consider disaster reporters as ambulance-chasing opportunists out to make bucks for their networks. Certainly, on the morning Rita struck, I heard one announcer promise, "This video reveals minor destruction, viewers, but let me *assure* you that as direct-hit footage becomes available, you'll see massive damage."

Better reporters, like Jennifer Mayerle from WKRG-TV in Mobile, Alabama, openly wept while interviewing people like Hardy Jackson, a man dazed by the loss of his wife, who slipped his grip when their house split in half. In catastrophes like this, the best reporters stay on to bring us stories of those who are suffering, so that we are able to resist the natural human tendency to tell ourselves that everything really is fine, just fine after all. They stay to tell us of looters juxtaposed with heroes who scoop up babies and golden retrievers from rooftops. They inspire us to give money for relief or to fill vans full of food and drive south.

Stellar reporters stay to reveal our own humanity in the midst of calamity. They stay to keep us real.

Because of their coverage of Katrina (embarrassing to federal and state officials and government agencies), assistance was at-the-ready for Rita. Because of their coverage, more than a million people evacuated in time for the next Big One. Hopefully, news reporting will keep the atrocities of how relief was mismanaged in public view long enough to make sure it never happens again.

When I initially visited the Big Easy twenty years earlier, it was love at first sight. I fell in love with its pluck, passion, and jazz steeped in a delicate broth seasoned by Creole culture and diversity. Bourbon Street (where "beads, breasts, and balconies come together"), voodoo potions, to-go cups breeding inebriation, and a rakish carelessness about keeping up the appearances of morality—these, too, define the nature of New Orleans.

Why am I, a Catholic middle-class college professor and mother of five, so attracted by this city whose lifestyle can be so unlike my own? Something in its Bohemian call, a call that declares anything is possible, appeals to my writer's self. If renegades and the righteous freely share the same streets, then I can write without borders. New Orleans inspires me to write free.

Only four months prior to Katrina, I was in New Orleans for professional reasons. My colleague Kent, our Ecuadorian student, Tania, and I attend conference sessions by day, but at night we are joined by Kent's wife, Ann, and by Jerry, who have each spent the day with their own appointments. Heading out into the larger city, I find the city's colorful celebrations a stark contrast to our sheetrock conference rooms. I am reminded anew of why I feel such kindred spirit with New Orleans. As excellent as the gumbo is where we sit on a balcony overlooking the Quarter, we are also entertained by a couple of mice running from hole to hole in the splintered floorboards of the restaurant. After dinner, we walk toward the sounds of blues and jazz pealing from nightclubs up the street.

Strains of the blues give way, however, as we stroll toward Decatur. Ann and Kent walk hand-in-hand as do Jerry and I. We are all clearly enchanted by the warm soft night. This is Tania's first time in New Orleans. Her classic Latina dark eyes and serious features break into easy laughter as we chat about the city's history. Although I have only seen Tania dressed in the traditional student garb— jeans, T-shirt, and tennis shoes—tonight she is decked out in a swirly black skirt, maroon V-neck sparkly blouse, and heels. She is dressed for "clubbing," and Kent, Ann, Jerry, and I have offered to escort her to where the young dance until the wee hours of the morning.

Friday night is Latin night at the House of Blues, and Issac Delgado's blend of samba and jazz slides out through the windows into the streets below our feet. Tania recognizes the song "O Estas Loca" and breaks into salsa steps on the cobbled sidewalk. "For the first time in the United States, I feel at home," she laughs. Tania enjoys Iowa, but the richer diversity of Louisiana is irresistible.

New Orleans has never been a polite town where varied cultures stick to tidy corners, each separated neatly from others. I gain a fresh appreciation through Tania's dance steps of the richness of this gumbo culture where everything is thrown into one pot and left to simmer—and sometimes boil over.

New Orleans is a place of acceptance, one without the pressure to adopt the lifestyles of others. You don't have to buy into everything here, but it's also not okay to judge those who are different from yourself. It is a place of Leave Well Enough Alone. As one cabbie tells me, "I don't drink, I don't womanize, I'm not superreligious. But in N'awlins, we don't tell others what to do. We just try to be civil and stay out of one another's way." It is the ultimate place of tolerance.

On my first visit, I heard worries about a city built "protected" by levees that can sustain only so much. I saw drawings demonstrating that if levees were to break, Lake Pontchartrain would flood and fill New Orleans like a bowl of soup. Back then, I wondered, "What if the Big One hits?" As inexpert as I am about hydrology and engineering, the obvious precarious position of a city below sea level, bordered on the north by Lake Pontchartrain and on the south by the Mississippi, is inescapable even to me. All the more reason I am outraged when President Bush tells Diane Sawyer on *Good Morning America*, "I don't think anybody anticipated the breach of levees."

Here on the Upper Mississippi, too, we know it's only a matter of time. Sooner or later, human engineering gives way as surely as jazz gives way to salsa at the House of Blues on a Friday night. As Mark Twain said a century earlier, "The Mississippi will always have its own way; no engineering skill can persuade it to do otherwise; it has always torn down the petty basketwork of the engineers and poured its giant floods whithersoever it chose."

The fragility of French Quarter eighteenth-century wooden buildings echoes the delicate balance we all shelter within ourselves. We want to believe we can, like broncobusters, break hurricanes and spring floods to a standstill by erecting levees, by drying up and by rebuilding. We want to believe in ways that defy logic that we can prevent IT from even happening.

We want to believe we are in charge. In fact, we are not.

I've been hosted by Army Corps of Engineers officials and their spouses in New Orleans as well as elsewhere and would be lying if I painted them as dastardly nature-haters. Most that I've met are well-informed, cultured, gracious people. Our local Corps lockmaster, Bill Hainstock, has spent hours teaching me about how dams function and about the satellite systems that assist the Corps in determining water levels among the many pools of the river. He's also helped me better understand the challenges of navigation, flooding, and restoration efforts.

One of the most cavernous gulfs between us naturalists and many engineers, however, is a philosophical one. Top-level Corps engineers imply repeatedly that if you build it high enough and wide enough, it'll hold when the Big One comes (however the Big One is defined for any given region). I find among them a pre–Aldo Leopold notion that the planet is ours to regulate, the rivers, ours to schedule and direct—in effect, "Go here, Mississippi, but not there. Be this deep, but not this deep. Don't spill over, whatever you do, don't spill over." Top Corps decision makers have a poor record when it comes to following the advice of scientists and hydrologists.

The past century of pumps, sandbags, wing dams, levees, floodwalls, and other structural failures find even engineers admitting that what was once cutting-edge is now outdated and likely to fail. Prior to the 1930s (when most of the locks and dams were built on the Upper Mississippi), engineers researched the world over for the newest, best technology. Even my trusty 1961 *World Book Encyclopedia* claims New Orleans is safeguarded against floods by "a great line of levees." More than seventy years after their construction, however, advances in the field prove that the cutting edge of the 1930s is more like a ragged cardboard blade.

Today the Corps also says the lock system is inefficient and that many miles of levees are likely to fail. The history of human interference—albeit well intended—is a startling reminder of how inept our efforts are in comparison to the ultimate power of nature.

In 1924, the Inner Harbor Navigation Canal (the Industrial Canal) opened. It connected the Mississippi to Lake Pontchartrain for the sake of commerce and industry. The Corps opened the Bonnet Carre Spillway in 1937. It acts as a release valve to be opened when the Mississippi River floods. The belief was that it would most certainly protect New Orleans from high water. In the 1950s, levees were built along the south shore of Lake Pontchartrain to protect the Orleans and Jefferson parishes from storm surges.

By 1963, the Mississippi River Gulf Outlet ("Mr. Go") opened to provide a shortcut for shipping from the Gulf of Mexico to New Orleans. It also allows saltwater to enter St. Bernard marshes and Lake Pontchartrain, resulting in the loss of freshwater marshes. Much of the St. Bernard wetlands have been destroyed in the process, wetlands that could have acted as sponges to absorb some of the high water.

Commerce, industry, retail establishments, and residential neighborhoods settled into areas supposedly protected by structures certified to keep them safe. But Katrina and Rita sent surges up Mr. Go and other engineered outlets and broke through levees, killing more than 1,000 people and leaving 374,000 people who had to evacuate the area homeless. Not only should Mr. Go be gone, but Mr. Go should also haunt any future attempts by the Corps to appease the barge industry's relentless drive for more engineering.

No one wanted it to turn out this way, but the tragic stories from New Orleans—coupled with our knowledge of how levees, floodwalls, and locks and dams have altered the ebb and flow of the entire river—must have a far greater impact on future engineering efforts than they have in the past. On the Upper Mississippi, the loss of wetlands and increased siltation of backwaters threaten places like Frentress Lake, which is currently filling in at the rate of one to six inches per year. The Corps and politicians at all levels have been warned for decades by scientists that what happened is exactly what was going to happen, but these experts have been largely ignored.

We can't just walk away from damaged levees and do nothing. Neither can we continue to allow people to be lured by the promise of dry land protected by structural engineering that will, sooner or later, give out. Not on the Upper Mississippi and most certainly not in places like New Orleans.

And yet there are signs of hope.

As I write today, Osty is building a new house next door here at Frentress Lake on the Mississippi backwaters. Before he was allowed to drive a single nail, however, the Corps, IEMA, the DNR, and the local community government coordinated to make sure the ground had been built up sufficiently to raise the house above the floodplain. Surveyors have to certify that the house's first floor will be elevated to a level higher than the one-hundred-year flood mark determined by the Corps based on statistics from past floods and storms.

Because our community decided to participate in FEMA's National Flood Insurance Program to get affordable flood insurance, residents must comply, or they can't build. Wray Childers, P.L.S. (at Iowa, Illinois, Wisconsin Engineers and Surveyors, P.C.) acknowledges that some folks complain about the regulations. Not me. Had such regulations been in place when my own house was built in the late 1980s, my husband and I would not face the prospect of being flooded out every five to ten years.

Upstream from us, Shore Acres—even more subject to flooding than we are—is undergoing phased FEMA buyouts because as a community they initiated the request and have agreed to regulations that come along with the buyouts. The city of East Dubuque, where Shore Acres resides, agreed to prevent the land from being purchased again only to have future residents face the same trauma. Folks there who have received a decent price for their homes are moving uphill voluntarily.

Authorities with the Illinois and Iowa emergency management agencies and departments of natural resources agree that 1993 was a pivotal year for flood mitigation efforts in this region. James Lee Witt was appointed head of FEMA, and he was the first FEMA director who had actual emergency mitigation experience. He shifted from depending upon structural ways to stop nature to more informed ways to work with nature to lessen devastation to both humans and the river.

In 1993, residents along the Upper Mississippi and Illinois rivers also incurred major damage. "Midwesterners are frugal people," Bill Cappuccio of the Iowa DNR tells me. "Instead of building lots of massive flood structures, people here realized after the flood of 1993 that sooner or later any structure put up against nature is going to break down. We shifted more to buyouts and other mitigation efforts." Illinois Energy Management Agency hazard mitigation specialist Rusty Tanton agrees: "We focus on both predisaster and postdisaster mitigation. It makes good sense to have buyouts, elevation, or relocation rather than helping people after it's too late and their homes are a mess."

The more officials I talk to from IEMA, DNR, and the Corps, the more I appreciate the charting, data-keeping, statistical engineering, research, and coordination they engage in on behalf of floodplain residents in these parts. The more I understand of how well they work together on the Upper Mississippi, the more heartache I feel, however, on behalf of the Gulf Coast.

Officials declare that the immensity of obliteration along the Gulf Coast makes full buyouts impossible. It's tied up in regulations over who had flood insurance, which parishes and wards complied with zoning, and which were relieved of regulations because they resided behind a "certified" levee. To complicate matters further, Louisiana politics get in the way of the kind of coordinated efforts we see on the Upper Mississippi, where strict zoning is enforced to prohibit building within floodplain areas.

Steve King, an Iowa congressman appointed to assist with reconstruction efforts in Louisiana, further explains, "Even if FEMA, DNR, and the Corps did their jobs perfectly, there'd be problems because corruption at city and state levels stands in the way of coordinating efforts with other agencies. Unless such political in-fighting can be restructured, there's little hope of permanent solutions for Louisiana."

This fills in much of the metaphorical gulf I experience in visiting New Orleans in the aftermath. Local citizens are relentless in blaming the government. Coverage by the *Times-Picayune,* interviews with people who stayed inside the city in September, and my own recollections of the weeks following Katrina have me agreeing with them. There can be no excusing the deplorably slow response while thousands of people were left abandoned by governmental agencies, organizations, and officials. The gulf I experience occurs, however, because the IEMA and DNR I know on the Upper Mississippi have achieved enormous success in dealing with flooding—particularly since making the philosophical shift from building floodwalls and levees to returning natural floodplains to the river through buyouts and zoning regulations.

Mindful that Katrina was "only" a category three hurricane when it hit much of Mississippi and Louisiana, I ask structural engineering experts, "What if the Corps builds the most advanced, strongest levees possible, and yet someday there's a hurricane at category six or even seven?" They respond that any newly constructed flood mitigation systems won't be able to handle it. Even those who remain unconvinced by scientific research on global warming and polar ice cap melt have to agree: how can anyone suppose that nature will stay tightly constricted within our human maximum seismic readings or category numbers?

As I write these words, the good news from New Orleans is that parish directors and city council members are ascending to roles of leadership in bringing their often disparate populations to unite for a common cause—namely, the permanent closing of Mr. Go. The *Times-Picayune* reports that Oliver Thomas, New Orleans City Council president, is urging, "If we don't stick together, we get what we deserve. I'm serious—white, black, blue, purple, chocolate, vanilla, pecan, Neapolitan, pralines 'n' cream, strawberry shortcake and rocky road." And for the first time, Congress has refused to fund dredging for Mr. Go.

In other hopeful news, Richard Wagonaar, commander of the Corps of Engineers' New Orleans district, tells *Scientific American,* "We are generally a lot more open than we were five or six years ago, especially with regard to environmental issues."

Meanwhile, my environmental activism on behalf of the Upper River has me attending and speaking at a series of Army Corps of Engineers public sessions to explain possible extension of locks and other navigational efforts. At one open session, I hear farmers claim that extended locks will be the savior of shipping for their grain to get to foreign markets and to keep them competitive internationally. I hear radicals claim that the Corps doesn't care about the environment "one iota." I hear claims on all sides that if only A, B, or C are done, the environment would be fine, just fine. But no one defines what "fine" means.

The effects of both flooding and navigational structures on the Upper Mississippi, as well as the hundreds of miles of levees below St. Louis, cause the backwaters to continue to fill and Louisiana coastal wetlands disappear at a rate of 25–35 square miles per year—that's equivalent to a football field every half hour. Hydrologists claim that storm surges could be reduced by one foot per square mile of wetlands (640 acres). Given that more than 1 million acres have been lost since the 1930s, simple math implies that the surge that came up from the Gulf through Mr. Go may have been harmless or even nonexistent had wetlands and marshes been intact.

I leave such Upper Mississippi River Corps sessions hungry for common sense. The National Academy of Sciences, a nonpartisan, nonprofit group of scientists and engineers, in reviewing the Corps' Waterway Feasibility Study, suggests nonstructural measures to alleviate traffic, such as scheduling barge arrivals and creating a system to reduce tow delays at the lock rather than depending upon the current practice of first-come, first-served. If trains can run on a schedule, thus preventing the need for building more tracks, can't expert barge tows do the same within reason? Such scheduling has proved successful for the Panama Canal and Saint Lawrence Seaway. The Environmental Defense Fund urges construction of mooring buoys, use of helper boats, and greater cooperation between tow operators as additional ways to reduce bank erosion and tree mortality. Such measures offer low-cost alternatives to extending locks and could be implemented almost immediately.

Corps data reveals there has been no increase in barge traffic on the Mississippi for two decades. Corps predictions for 1992–2001 contrast with actual traffic patterns by as much as 12.5 million tons.

Inflation of traffic predictions has plagued the Corps and the lock extension issue for years—all the more reason that nonstructural methods are likely to work and should be tried before extending current locks. Will the Corps do as science suggests?

There's a great deal to be gained by trying out nonstructural measures—$1.2 billion or more, the current price tag for extending locks—to say nothing of creating a healthier environment for the river and the people who use it.

Tania, Kent, Ann, Jerry, and I sip chicory café au lait and breakfast on beignets at Café Du Monde, the powdered sugar sifting onto my black dress slacks. We roam the French Quarter, and I spend an afternoon laughing and knitting with the wild women at the Quarter Stitch yarn shop on Chartres Street.

I sample Creole Gulf shrimp at Emeril's ("Bam!") and stroll the waterfront watching enormous barges and ocean vessels maneuver along the Mississippi, which curves to cradle New Orleans. I do not know it yet, but four months later, such vessels will be used to deliver hundreds of FEMA trailers for those left homeless by hurricanes. But this is pre-Katrina, so I am left to bask in the pleasantries of watching boats move through the crescent.

There's no city quite like it—remarkable considering that before New Orleans was a city, it was swampland. In fact, geologists once called it "a land between earth and sea, belonging to neither and alternately claimed by both." Perhaps it was always meant to be of water.

About a thousand miles upstream, our own river house hosted the Mississippi for six weeks during the flood of 2001. Mice carcasses decorated the living room. We shoveled dead catfish out of the basement. Receding mud left rings around the walls and caked our kitchen floor, but these were the least of it.

What got into the joists and studs invited mold and rot. We tore out and replaced, but we were far from having the whole house floating downriver. Like New Orleans built on marsh, this house was built on a floodplain.

For the past few years, the spring rise has stayed politely in the basement, so my daydreams are filled with the grandest American river rolling by my front door; but my nightmares are awash with rising tides. In December, as snowflakes accumulate to a foot or more, friends who live atop the bluffs appreciate the poetry and design of winter's first demonstration. I am preoccupied, however, by images of spring melt flowing down mountainsides, into tributaries, into the river, and flooding into my kitchen. Each rain storm sends me searching the Web to check river levels in Prairie Du Chien, LaCrosse, and St. Paul.

Ironically, we experience remarkably low water on the Upper Mississippi while Katrina pummels into the coast. As I stand on our beached dock, looking south I am struck by the differences between Gulf residents and me even though we share a shoreline.

At best, those who lived in Lakeside, parts of the Garden District, and other middle-class or wealthy regions did so because they believed enough in the levees of New Orleans to feel safe. Without tightly enforced elevation restrictions, that's how communities develop behind floodwalls and levees. Because there's no earthen levee between me and the Mississippi, I feel no such assurance.

I *choose* to live here—unlike many of my neighbors upstream at Shore Acres, Illinois, as well as those downstream, flooded out by Katrina and Rita. For many who live along the water's edge, these lowlands are the least expensive properties available. It's the only affordable place. With no cars or bank accounts, and no membership in America's dominant majority class, such river dwellers are often left to the sporadic charity of others, unreliable government relief services, or to blind luck.

When the Big One hits my neighborhood, however, my family and I will toss photo albums and memorabilia into boxes, carry them out to the dinghy tied to the back door, paddle to our cars on higher ground, and leave. We may all live on floodplains, but the tragic gulf between people like me and my lower Ninth Ward New Orleans fellow Americans is one called choice.

Shore Acres, like a miniature version of New Orleans, was built in a bowl, threatened on several sides by the Mississippi and Lake Lakoma. Now they have the choice to accept buyouts and move uphill.

As I write this final chapter to this book about dreaming of the Mississippi as its once-wild self, I'm in New Orleans taping interviews and touring areas hit hardest by waters that rose beyond human ability to contain them. The irony is profoundly sad and impossible for me to sort out because I am so deeply moved by those I meet. It seems surreal that it has been months since Katrina and its tragic aftermath.

On this current visit to New Orleans, I am with a group of museum officials including an artist, a riverboat captain, an engineer, a mayor, a lawyer, an antique shop owner, a museum director, and a journalist who covered the Mississippi River flood of 1965. This leisure trip—including a jaunt down to Pilot Town by boat—was planned back before hurricane season. When we offer to cancel our visit, given conditions in the region, officials assure us that they strongly prefer we come anyway, "So you can see for yourself and tell others."

I spend the first day in the delightful French Quarter dining on po'boy sandwiches at Mother's, frequenting shops, and hanging out at Quarter Stitch Yarns.

"My house in St. Bernard Parish will be bulldozed," one of the yarn women says. "But my FEMA trailer arrived last week and once they inspect it—in a month or so—I get to move in." Exchanging yarns on Katrina around the big table, one woman recalls finding shelter in a hotel during the storm. She recounts, "I kept the blinds closed, but I could hear the building creaking in the wind and feel it swaying. After it was over and the water came up, I could hear people in the night calling out to be saved. I couldn't help them. Sometimes now I wake up in the middle of the night and imagine that I still hear them calling."

As we click away, knitting socks, shawls, and caps, I notice the slim woman to my left is noticeably quiet. She pats the top of her chestnut hair anxiously as she speaks. She looks up from her knitting and arrests my attention with her intensity and her blue-green eyes that become watery as she speaks, "I only recently returned from Texas. Christmas was hard. I saw Katrina books on the sale tables. After three months, we'd become 'remainders.'"

Most of the locals I interview worry that America has forgotten.

Like Upper Mississippi River residents who have been flooded out repeatedly, these Louisiana residents often highlight a common lesson they learned in surviving: "You can depend upon yourself, maybe your neighbors, and if you're lucky, kind strangers."

Most agree that the quickest and most generous relief comes from volunteer efforts. Our own Clarke College students spent the last week of Christmas break in the region, assigned to individual

families whom they assist in cleaning up rubble and sorting be-
longings. More will return during subsequent breaks. Other college
students—strongly encouraged by Iowa congressman Leonard
Boswell—also make several service trips to Mississippi to volunteer through churches. Graceland College participates. The New
Orleans Steamboat Company thanks volunteers by offering free
rides on the steamer *Natchez.* Habitat for Humanity, Catholic Relief
Services, the Red Cross, and other organizations attend to crucial
needs of housing and food.

Church groups and preachers who spontaneously filled vans with
food and bottled water and drove south are tops on the praise list
of locals. One cabbie tells of a Texas preacher and his congregation
taking in dozens of hurricane victims, "They kept feeding us and
listening to us. I have never experienced such goodness. Next
month I'm retiring and will volunteer full time with the church."

When I ask everyone—from cabbies to doormen to waitstaff to
booksellers to Harbor police—what message I should carry north,
answers vary from finger-pointing (George Bush, FEMA, Louisiana
politicians, the Corps, and one man's mother-in-law) to inspiring
stories of rescue to finding God. I hear two requests repeatedly. At
first they seem contradictory.

Don't forget us.

Outside of tourist areas, vast regions like St. Bernard Parish and
the Ninth Ward are still without electricity, water, or cleanup as of
this writing. I see houses that were tossed into the middle of inter-
sections and streets splattered with boats, dolls, chairs, photographs, mattresses, and messages painted on crestfallen houses
telling where former inhabitants can be located.

Occasionally we come across owners sifting through rubble, but
even these efforts are severely regulated or even prohibited in many
areas because dilapidated structures are too precarious to enter. In
a heavily settled residential lower Ninth Ward neighborhood, I
squint up into the afternoon sun and realize that as far as the eye
can gaze, I cannot find a single standing structure.

Not one.

Walk down the Main Street of your city. As you do, imagine finding nothing higher than four feet—no quaint coffee shops, no hotels
named after city founders, no art centers and museums, no cozy

historic houses tucked in here and there, no banks, no specialty restaurants, not even a McDonalds. No Town Clock. No trees. Instead your gaze is met by massive amounts of rubble and debris, most of it barely recognizable as parts of the buildings and homes you once knew well. As you drive uphill to where schools, churches, and homes once stood, you still find nothing recognizable—only piles of bricks, twisted school buses, crushed houses, trash, and artifacts of private lives strewn all the way to the outermost suburbs.

"Bodies Possible," appears red-painted on one house. Joe Labarriere, our Harbor Police guide, confirms that bodies are likely still inside. A child's hobby horse stands ten feet away.

We continue as Joe drives the van south toward Venice, the southernmost Louisiana point reachable by car. I discover dozens of levee breaks, one with a barge sitting atop it. Heaps of mangled cars, roofs crushed down upon trucks, and enormous mounds of rotting refrigerators line the highway. Although there are seven of us in the car, a stillness falls over us as we revere those whose utter devastation spreads out beyond our car windows as far as the eye can see. I cannot even guess the number of square miles.

Whether a house was flooded or not, it was without electricity for weeks or months. Refrigerators were removed from the Quarter and other tourist areas, but not before residents exhibited their typical Louisianan sense of the macabre by painting messages on them: "Free Food," "Katrina Leftovers," "Free Gumbo Inside," and "Big Nasty." Pickup hasn't extended this far south, however. Some refrigerators are closed with duct tape, others stand open and filthy. Since many contain Freon, disposal is wrought with environmental worries.

"It looks like a war zone," Joe comments. I grimace at the horrific irony. Louisiana alone is paying $2.1 billion for the Iraq war; that's equivalent to 26,975 housing units. Nationally, the $240 billion war price tag equates to over two million housing units.

How can we spend so much money destroying life and so little restoring it?

The *Times-Picayune* reports that only 11 percent of House and Senate members have visited these areas, yet these officials will vote on recovery aid and reconstruction plans. Without seeing it themselves, will these officials be left to depend upon news photos to convey the enormity of obliteration? That would be like expecting a postage stamp image of the Grand Canyon to render reality.

Structure flipped by hurricane Katrina.

Katrina aftermath.

The author at Pilot Town, Louisiana, with
aftermath of Katrina behind her.

Later, when President Bush visits for the first time in over three
months, he claims, "We've come a long way in four months." I suspect homeless folks from St. Bernard Parish and the lower Ninth
Ward would disagree. The president's motorcade drives past very
little of the destruction, however, so he and I see two vastly different
versions of New Orleans. Viewing the French Quarter, the Garden
District, and Lakeside, it's easy to believe New Orleans has already
made a comeback. That's why it's crucial for government officials
to visit, since they will vote to determine funding for cleanup, reconstruction, and what to do about the levee system.

The second thing the Katrina survivors keep telling me is, *Come
to New Orleans.*

President Bush is right, however, when he claims New Orleans is
"One heck of a place to take your family." There's never been a better time to visit. The crime rate is nearly nil. Without the usual
crowds, it's easy to get tables at all dining establishments.

After my travel companions and I feast on scrumptious beignets
at Café Du Monde, we cross the street to where carriages await
tourists. We meet the driver of a mule-drawn carriage, "I'm Bertrand
Coleman, always imitated, but never duplicated." As he smiles, the

Awaiting beignets at Café Du Monde.

Sign in French Quarter shop.

Bertrand Coleman with the author.

morning sun glints off his gold front tooth. He speaks jauntily, rhyming at every turn, but in his eyes I think I detect a sadness caused by the heartache of the past months. Bertrand's rugged features and weathered face suggest a life of hard work and struggle. He urges me to climb onto the carriage: "Come on you writer-girl, git on up here, and let's have them take our picture, so I can get a little African color into your photos!" Bertrand tells us that he is a famous hoofer known throughout New Orleans; his worn leather shoes testify to his dancing days. Taking the reins, he also introduces us to his mule, "Janet Jackson." With his beret cocked to the right side of his head, he strokes his goatee and we are off.

Bertrand tours us by Jackson Square, the Cabildo, the Aquarium of the Americas, a former slaves auction site, and the movie location for Elvis's elementary school. All the while, he rhymes incessantly and pleasantly. Occasionally, he turns to his mules, snaps the reins, "Git on up there," without losing the cadence of his tour-guide shtick. At the Gazebo Café, Bertrand whoas the mules and hops out of the carriage. "I'm going to show you something you won't see anywhere else," he calls up to us and begins dancing alongside jazz street musicians. By the time the song ends, Bertrand's fancy footwork has attracted a crowd, who applaud as he returns to the driver's seat.

Signs of hope.

The French Quarter returns.

Bertrand dancing in the streets of New Orleans.

Later his eyes fill as he explains that his daughter was found only yesterday—four months after Katrina. She is alive.

The French Quarter is 90 percent intact; hotels, restaurants, and attractions are charming and festive. By the time this book is in your hands, the Quarter will be in even better shape. The city's comeback depends partly upon tourism, so spending is guilt-free. You're helping our neighbors downriver. And the gumbo is even better than ever for the realization that we may have lost this cultural delicacy.

The sunset view of the Mississippi is breathtaking. Theaters are back in lively operation, prices are low, powdered sugar still snows down from beignets, and Mother's is open. Best of all, Bertrand is dancing.

Just as hurricane season descends upon the southern United States, rising Mississippi tides may well be making their way through my house. When the river rises this spring, my husband and I will once again descend the stairs outside in the moonlight, open the basement doors, and lift our wine glasses to the river, "Good night Mississippi." But this year I'll add, "I'm keeping the light on for you, New Orleans."

Landlubber's Lexicon

Aft, boaters will tell you, refers to the stern. In plain language, that's the back of the boat, folks!

Backwaters serve as crucial parts of the river ecosystem. Because they filter the river and provide haven for waterfowl and numerous species of animals and insects along with flora and fauna, the backwaters also are home to the most heavenly spots on the planet. Wayne Norman, a wise friend of mine, often said, "The genius of the Mississippi is in the backwaters."

Bajas are sleek, fast boats that skim across water as if they're gliding on air. They're beautiful, but they boast that they move so fast, everything goes by in a blur. Some of us like to see where we're going.

Berth might suggest a sleeping space on board, but here I use it to suggest a safe space between towboat and other boats. Give towboats a wide berth. Trust me on this.

Bottom feeders do just that — they feed off the bottom of rivers and other ponds. Catfish are among my favorites. Like other bottom feeders, their location is predictable; they prefer the downside of wing dams and deeper, darker waters.

Bows might refer to a bend at the waist that performers take, but on the river, the bow is the front of the boat. Hopefully, it doesn't bend at the waist.

Bubble in is the wonderfully pictorial term applied to how boats are kept in water in northern regions despite advancing ice. A "bubbler" motor is attached to either the boat or dock to keep water churning. Churning water can't freeze. (Milwaukee natives like me, however, insist that bubblers are drinking fountains.)

Channel: on the river, this has nothing to do with California whoo-whoo ESP or talking to the dead. Instead, the noun refers to the main channel of the Mississippi River where the Army Corps of Engineers maintains a nine-foot depth so that towboats and smaller craft can navigate along this main corridor. On the weekends, with heavier traffic, the main channel is a good place to avoid.

Channelize, to some on the Mississippi, is a verb full of magic because it ensures that boats can get up- or downstream. Environmentally, however, channelizing is a nightmare, since the dredging and damming required to channelize have also resulted in the loss of habitat for wildlife and river ecology.

Cigarette boats are thus named for their long, sleek appearance. Also referred to as *cigar boats,* they extend in the bow like those great big old stogies that your granddad (or grandma) used to smoke.

Crawdaddy is our native lingo for crayfish. "Crawdaddies" sound cuter and a lot tastier than crayfish.

Crick-stomping, creek stomping: slogging through the backwaters, usually scavenging for "treasures" such as antique bottles, boat bumpers, five-legged frogs, or clay. Because there may be reeds, knee-deep water, and mud, one must "stomp" more than "walk."

Cub pilot is a lot like a bear cub. She knows a lot, but not nearly as much as the lead pilot, so she signs on to intern with her.

Cuddy is a cozy, small space on a yacht or boat which pretends to be a bedroom. You might equate it to a loft or unfinished attic.

Cut does not refer to a scissors or a nasty remark on the river. An often slim corridor with fast current, a cut connects the main channel to backwater sloughs. In low water, some cuts disappear altogether because land emerges solid to the shore. During high water, when swifter currents carry fallen trees and debris downstream, cuts often get snaggy and downright ornery. Experienced boaters on the Mississippi know to approach cuts cautiously once flood waters recede; you never know what may have lodged down there, waiting to rip off your hull or snarl the prop.

DNR (Department of Natural Resources) is the state government agency whose mission is to protect the environment of the river as well as promote fishing and hunting. One of the DNR's greatest services on the Mississippi is to keep humankind from destroying the riparian and from polluting the Big River.

Draw, in river talk, has nothing to do with Picasso. Instead, it measures how deep an engine churns underwater or how low a keel sits. Most recreation boats have a draw of about 18 inches. More shallow ones (like canoes and johnboats) might only draw 6 inches, whereas deeper boats (yachts, tows) might draw 2 to 3 feet. Knowing your boat's draw is important before entering shallow backwaters. Before entering, it's common for a boater to call out to another on the pond, "How much is the draw in there?"

Dredging makes shallow (shoal) waters navigable. Big vacuum tubes, which scoop up sand and silt and unmentionables at the river bottom, keep the channel and cuts deep enough for boats. Marinas often dredge the cuts and sloughs to boat docks to keep slip renters happy.

FEMA (Federal Emergency Management Agency) has undergone numerous challenges in assisting flood victims since 1979. Local chapters like IEMA (which designates either the Iowa or Illinois Emergency Management Agency) work in full recognition that no one can really control the river. In areas of the Upper Mississippi that flood frequently, nowadays IEMA works with local communities to authorize buyouts, to undevelop the land, and to return floodplains to the river. In doing so, human misery is prevented and the environmental mistakes of the past are slowly being corrected. In earlier times, levees and floodwalls were built instead, but we're learning our lessons (I hope).

Floodwalls are impenetrable fortresses of concrete that protect cities and farmlands from the Mississippi's powerful floods. However, they also cause water to rise higher and more forcefully further downstream until the lower river suffers irreparable damage, loss of wetlands, and ultimate desecration. For the most part, these were constructed back when we didn't know any better. "Something there is that doesn't love a wall," Robert Frost claims. I'm with him on this one.

Forward is the mariner's opposite of *aft*. It refers to the front of a boat.

Houseboats are the ultimate metaphor for American nomadic life. They range from being glamorous, multimillion-dollar, five-bedroom, ultramodern, air-conditioned yachts to homemade shacks constructed of plywood nailed to a frame made of driftwood. Despite the disparity, they boast in common owners who can't get enough of the Mississippi. Many houseboaters vacation for weekends or a whole week now and again. There are also those who hole up for the season, bragging that they haven't stood on terra firma for months.

Johnboats are favored by fishers because they have less draw and thus can maneuver in the backwaters where fish are often more plentiful. Although luxury johnboats with leather seats are occasionally spotted on the river, most of them running past our stretch of the river are green or silver with bench seats and a couple of chair-seats that sit higher in order to better position the fisher. They're great for an easy run on the river. I've been asking for one for Christmas for years.

Larboard used to mean the "loading side" of a boat, but it's now used generally to refer to the left side as you face the front of the boat. Instead of asking for a line to be tossed to the larboard side, however, most of us just say, "Throw me a line. I'm stuck in the mud (again)."

Levees can be overcome regularly by high water—more regularly than residents are promised by those who design them. There's a levee system on the Mississippi running for hundreds of miles. Like a girdle holding in girth, levee embankments are designed to hold in floodwater. While this may result in dryer towns, it wreaks havoc on the environment. Wetlands that provided habitat to many species have also dried up. High water can't spill onto natural floodplains, so the toxicity in the river builds up until all the chemicals and hog runoff flows down past New Orleans into what has now been termed the Dead Zone and Cancer Alley. Ring levees that "ring" a town, thus allowing water to spill everywhere else, are far kinder to the environment and ultimately to humans.

Line is the term for "rope" on a boat, as in: "Please tie the line to the dock." But if you call it a "rope" by mistake, I'm sure the deck-hand will tie it for you anyway.

Locks and dams have been built alongside one another by the Army Corps of Engineers since the 1930s to hold water back in order to ensure a nine-foot channel in each pool. Commonly misperceived, locks and dams were not built to control floods. Because of the lock and dam system, the Upper Mississippi is actually a series of pools rather than a continuous flowing river. Dams are numbered, beginning with #1 at St. Anthony's Falls, at St. Paul, down to #27, at Alton near St. Louis. There are twenty-nine of them (don't ask about the those two missing numbers; you don't want to know). The dams are the end "walls" of the pools. The locks provide a means by which boats can move up- and downstream without having to leapfrog the walls. The water level is higher upstream than it is downstream. Much like watery elevators, the pool in each lock raises and lowers to accommodate boats progressing to the next level. Boats enter through a gate (lock) on one end of the pool, the lock closes, and the water is raised or lowered, depending on whether you're moving up- or downstream. Once the water level reaches the same height as the next pool, the gate at the other side of the chamber is opened, and boats go on their merry little way. During floods, the gates are left completely open to allow water to flow through.

Locking through refers to moving through a lock chamber, as in "I'm locking through at dam #11."

Mud is the most common river bottom material. After a while, you get used to it.

Pool, on the Mississippi north of St. Louis, refers to a stretch of river between two dams (see *Locks and dams*). Pool numbers correspond to dam numbers.

Put in is the verb boaters use for the process of getting a boat into water. One might say, "I *put in* at Dubuque" or more specifically, "I *put in* at Mid-town Marina." As a noun, the term might be used to designate the place where this activity occurs: "Where's the closest *put-in?*"

Quimby's Cruising Guide advises boaters about restaurants, dockage, marinas, and other crucial information on the Mississippi, Illinois, Missouri, Ohio, Arkansas, and many other rivers.

Rec boat stands for *recreation boat*. I've never heard rec boaters refer to themselves as such, but lock masters use the term. Someone has to distinguish between those of us who are out there for fun and those who are working the barges.

Ring levees, kinder than miles of straight levees, provide protection from floods by forming a "ring" around a town or farm; this maintains more wetlands and floodplains, allowing the Mississippi to spill.

River rat is one of the most disputed terms river people use. Some reserve the term for only those old grizzled guys who hang out in bayous and swamps, refusing to talk to anyone but a bullhead. A few use the term as synonymous with a no-account ne'er-do-well, the bottom feeders of humankind. Most of us use *river rat* to refer to anyone who loves the Mississippi, someone who just can't wait to get out there.

Runabout is a generic term applied to recreation boats.

Shoal water indicates places where the river is shallow. Sometimes this is due to a sandbar rising from the bottom of the river.

Silt is soil that runs off into the Mississippi and is carried downstream. Because of floodwalls and the levee system, which prevent silt from flooding onto floodplains, the river suffers a disastrous buildup of this sedimentation, which is beginning to fill up even the backwaters.

Slip: if yours is showing, on the river, it's a good thing. Slips are rented boat spaces connected by docks at marinas. Using the word as a verb, boaters might ask one another, "Where do you slip your boat?"

Slough is a term commonly used as nearly synonymous with *backwater*. Generally shallower than the main channel, the current is slower in sloughs. Sloughs are the favored corridors for nature-loving canoeists, kayakers, and small-boat boaters. In recent years, jet skiers, too, have taken to sloughing. Although the motors that propel those small craft aren't powerful, jet skis produce a horrendous wallop, polluting the air with noise and destroying shoreline habitat. Hopefully officials along the Mississippi will protect the quietude of these backwaters by enacting the same legislation as Minnesota's boundary waters: No jet skis! (I'm sorry, river kids, that's what I think and I'm sticking to it.)

Snag is anything that threatens your prop or your bare feet. Snags might be nature's work (fallen branches or clumps of mud and foliage) or the result of human ineptitude (things thrown in the river like rusted lawn mowers or mangled lawn furniture).

Snag boats, invented by Henry Shreve in the 1930s, operated with enormous hooks that could snag tree trunks and debris and move them out of the river, thus making the channel safer for navigation.

Starboard is the right-hand side as you face the front of a boat.

Steering sticks, rather than a wheel, are what pilots on towboats and big excursion boats use. These four-foot "poles" extend horizontally toward the captain.

Stern refers to the back of a boat. It's the opposite of the forward. Many of the charming paddlewheel boats from the nineteenth century were stern-wheelers—boats with their paddles at the back.

Sticks. See *Steering sticks*

Stump fields lurk underwater on the main channel and backwaters. Named for stumps left over when the land was clear-cut in years when water was lower, the term is usually applied to any area full of dead wood or fallen branches.

Switchback refers to places where the course of the Mississippi does a hairpin turn, usually 180 degrees (more or less).

Throttle down indicates that a pilot is running the boat at full-speed.

Tubing has gained popularity during the last decade and now competes with water skiing as one of the chief sports on the river. Anyone can do it. A heavy vinyl or rubberized ring attached to a good strong line is towed behind the boat. Sitting in or hanging onto the tube is a *tuber*. Tubers, while often children, are frequently of the adult variety. Being a tuber is far better than being a couch potato!

Wing dams are underwater brush and stone walls extending from the riverbank toward the channel, usually at a 90-degree angle. Built close together, often with only a few hundred feet between them, there are thousands on the river. Although these structures were built more than a hundred years ago, they're still common on the Upper Mississippi. In low water, wing dams are the bane of boaters, who risk propeller and keel unless they attend to river charts.

Bibliography

American Rivers, Inc. *In Harm's Way: A Report on Floods and Flood Plains*. Washington, D.C.: American Rivers Publications, 1999.

Barnes, Gerald. "Maintaining the Inland Waterway System for Agricultural Shippers." Speech at the Agricultural Outlook Forum, Omni Shoreham Hotel, Washington, D.C., Tuesday, February 24, 1998. http://www.usda.gov/oce/waob/Archives/1998/speeches/076/BARNES.DOC.

Boland, Thomas. "A Classification of Wing and Closing Dams on the Upper Mississippi River Bordering Iowa." Report to the Fish and Wildlife Management Work Group of GREAT II. Des Moines: Iowa Conservation Commission, 1980.

Buzan, David. As quoted in "In Storm's Wake, Estuary Day Shows Value of Wetlands." http://www.tpwd.state.tx.us/newsmedia/releases/?req=20051003a, January 12, 2006.

Capuccio, William. Personal Interview. January 25, 2006.

Center for Global Education of Hamline University. "Mississippi Feature: Pollution." http://cgee.hamline.edu/rivers/Resources/Feature/feat7.htm, January 15, 2006.

Childers, Wray. Personal Interview. January 19, 2006.

Cowan, Walter, Charles Dufour, John Chase, O. K. LeBlanc, and John Wilds. *New Orleans: Yesterday and Today*. Baton Rouge: Louisiana State University Press, 1983.

Ellis, William. "The Mississippi: River under Siege." *National Geographic* 184, no. 5A (1993): 90–105.

Environmental Defense Fund. http://www.environmentaldefense.org/home.cfm, December 27, 2005.

Faber, Scott. *The Real Choices Report: The Failure of America's Flood Control Policies*. Washington, D.C.: American Rivers Publications, 1995.

Fischetti, Mark. "Protecting New Orleans." *Scientific American*, February 2006, 64–71.

Fremling, Calvin R. *Immortal River: The Upper Mississippi in Ancient and Modern Times*. Madison: University of Wisconsin Press, 2005.

Grunwald, Michael. "Engineers of Power: An Agency of Unchecked Clout." *Washington Post*, September 10, 2000, AO1–AO3.

Hainstock, William. Personal Interview. September 14, 2005, and January 23, 2006.

Lake Pontchartrain Basin Foundation. http://www.saveourlake.org/, January 20, 2006.

Levins, Richard, Philip Rice, and Elizabeth Swain. *Will It Really Help Farmers? The Upper Mississippi River Navigation Project*. Minneapolis: Institute for Agriculture and Trade Policy, 2000.

Martin, Glen. "Wetland Restoration Seen as Crucial." *San Francisco Chronicle*, September 5, 2006. http://www.sfgate.com/cgi-bin/article.cgi?f=/c/a/2005/09/05/MNG69EIHUK1.DTL, November 5, 2006.

McLeod, Reggie. "Did the Corps Cook the Books?" *Big River*, March 2000. http://www.big-river.com/cookbooks.html.

———. "Marketing Lock Expansion." *Big River*, July–August 2004, 15–49.

Mississippi River Basin Alliance. http://www.mrba.org/.

National Oceanic and Atmospheric Administration (U.S. Department of Commerce). http://www.noaa.gov/, October 12, 2005.

National Priorities Project. "Iraq War Count." http://national priorities.org/index.php?option=com;wrapper&Itemid=182, January 23, 2006.

National Research Council, Committee to Review the Corps of Engineers Restructured Upper Mississippi River–Illinois Waterway Feasibility Study. *Review of the U.S. Army Corps of Engineers Restructured Upper Mississippi River–Illinois Waterway Feasibility Study: Second Report*. Washington, D.C.: National Academies Press, 2004.

National Weather Service. River Watch Mississippi River Basin. http://www.riverwatch.noaa.gov/forecasts/DVNRVDDVN .shtml, January 16, 2006.

Outwater, Alice. *Water: A Natural History.* New York: Basic Books, 1996.

Palmer, Tim. *Lifelines: The Case for River Conservation.* Washington, D.C.: Island Press, 1994.

Petersen, William. "Mississippi River Floods." *Palimpsest* 46 (July 1965): 305–64.

Tanton, Russell. Personal Interview. January 24, 2006.

Tidwell, Mike. *Bayou Farewell: The Rich Life and Tragic Death of Louisiana's Cajun Coast.* New York: Pantheon, 2003.

Twain, Mark. *Adventures of Huckleberry Finn.* New York: Bantam, 1981.

———. *Life on the Mississippi.* New York: Bantam, 1985.

———. *Mark Twain in Eruption: Hitherto Unpublished Pages about Men and Events.* Ed. Bernard DeVoto. New York: Harper, 1940.

U.S. Army Corps of Engineers. "Status of Locks and Dams: Controlling Clearances in Mississippi River Pools." http://www2 .mvr.usace.army.mil/NavNotices/ Documents/DBIIStats2005 Master1.pdf.

U.S. Environmental Protection Agency. "National Estuary Program." http://www.epa.gov/owow/estuaries/coastlines/oct02/ americorps.html, January 28, 2006.

White House Conference on Cooperative Conservation. "Strengthening Shared Government and Citizen Stewardship." http:// conservation.ceq.gov/agenda.html, August 31, 2005.

Williams, Leslie. "Eastern N.O. Residents Call for MR-GO to Close." *New Orleans Times-Picayune,* January 28, 2006. http://www .nola.com/newslogs/tpupdates/index.ssf?/mtlogs/ nola_tpupdates/archives/2006_01_28.html#108492, January 29, 2006.

Williams, Terry Tempest. *Refuge: An Unnatural History of Family and Place.* New York: Vintage, 1992.

Questions and Discussion Guide

1. In "Itasca," the author notes that the book does not follow chronological order. How might the book have been different if Fischer had followed sequential order?

2. Discuss causes of environmental damage to the Mississippi chronicled within the book.

3. Relate concerns of flooding and human intervention with the river to recent natural catastrophes in the news. What similarities do you find?

4. Discuss stereotypes of the Mississippi and how *Dreaming the Mississippi* offers alternatives to such myths.

5. Although the author points a finger at others for wreaking havoc on the river, in what ways does she acknowledge her own guilt when it comes to interfering with nature?

6. "Talk of allowing nature to take its own course levels social class barriers and makes country and city dwellers, often at odds with one another, close as two kernels on a cob of Iowa sweet corn." Find experiences from the book that support the author's assertion.

7. "Brine" and "Sho-Gunning the Mississippi" take readers away from the shores of the Mississippi. What perspectives do these off-location chapters offer?

8. In Mark Twain's *The Adventures of Huckleberry Finn,* Huck often goes to the river to escape the struggles and complexities of city life. In what ways does Fischer find similar refuge on the Mississippi?

9. The hunt for a river residence is one of numerous everyday events exaggerated in the book. Note others. Discuss what is gained through such exaggeration.

10. Fischer rarely misses an opportunity to create metaphors, coin new phrases, and play with language. Discuss the effects on the book overall as a result of these language acrobatics.

11. Compare *Dreaming the Mississippi* with other "Sense of Place" books.

12. Throughout the book, the author grapples not only with environmental issues, but also with the concerns of a mother, teacher, citizen, and writer. In what ways does she find answers or resolve such concerns?

13. Discuss the sense of celebration and carpe diem that permeates much of the book.

About the Author

Katherine Fischer is Associate Professor of English at Clarke College, a consultant to the National Mississippi River Museum and Aquarium, and a newspaper columnist. She lives on both sides of the Mississippi—atop river bluffs in Dubuque, Iowa, and on the floodplain of a backwater slough at Frentress Lake, Illinois.

Photo by Andrew Enzler